"Sameet Kumar's *Mindfulness and Prolonged Grief Work*
tant resource for both those struggling to cope with prolo
the helping professionals who are advising and supporting

—**Sharon Salzberg**, author of *Real Happiness* and *Lovingkindness*

"Sameet Kumar has been working for many years as a psychologist and counselor in the field of dealing with this grief. In his wonderful new book *Mindfulness and Prolonged Grief*, he shares many of the approaches to inner healing that he has developed in his practice. In particular, he demonstrates how the ancient Buddhist methods of mindfulness meditation can be used to cure both body and mind when the overwhelming darkness of grief, depression, and hopelessness sets in. His book is both practical and immediate in its presentation, offering medical practitioners and patients alike a clear guide to a traditional healing technology that has worked for centuries, and is perhaps even more relevant today than ever before."

—**Glenn Mullin**, author of *Living in the Face of Death* and *The Fourteen Dalai Lamas: A Sacred Legacy of Reincarnation*

mindfulness
for
prolonged grief

◆ ◆ ◆

a guide to healing after loss when
depression, anxiety, and anger won't go away

SAMEET M. KUMAR, PhD

New Harbinger Publications, Inc.

Distributed in Canada by Raincoast Books

Copyright © 2013 by Sameet M. Kumar
New Harbinger Publications, Inc.
5674 Shattuck Avenue
Oakland, CA 94609
www.newharbinger.com

Cover design by Amy Shoup
Text design by Michele Waters-Kermes
Acquired by Catharine Meyers
Edited by Jasmine Star

Library of Congress Cataloging-in-Publication Data

Kumar, Sameet M.
  Mindfulness for prolonged grief : a guide to healing after loss when depression, anxiety, and anger won't go away / Sameet M. Kumar, PhD.
      pages cm
  Includes bibliographical references.
  ISBN 978-1-60882-749-7 (pbk. : alk. paper) -- ISBN 978-1-60882-750-3 (pdf e-book) -- ISBN 978-1-60882-751-0 (epub) 1. Grief. 2. Loss (Psychology) 3. Meditation--Therapeutic use. 4. Grief--Religious aspects. I. Title.
  BF575.G7K863 2013
  155.9'37--dc23

                          2013033444

Printed in the United States of America

15   14   13

10   9   8   7   6   5   4   3   2   1

First printing

This book is dedicated to the universal capacity for love and to all those who work to increase the unconditional love we have for each other.

Sarve mangalam. May all beings everywhere be happy.

Contents

Foreword

Many years ago I had the opportunity to visit a very unusual monastery in Thailand. In virtually every room there were human skulls, skeletons, and pictures of dead bodies. Periodically the monks performed autopsies on local people who had died and donated their bodies to the monastery. They weren't studying medicine, however. Instead, the monks performed autopsies to experience in a very real way that we are all made of flesh and blood, and that we all die. While I didn't get to know the monks well, they clearly weren't disturbed or depressed. Rather, they were smiling and energetic, seeming to go about their days fully engaged in the activity of the moment, appreciating life. The monks were practicing mindfulness—living each day richly, continually aware that life on earth is a finite series of fleeting moments.

It is striking how most of us living in the developed world are surprised by death. We go about our lives thinking of reasons death happens to other people, not to us or our loved ones. So when it strikes close to home, we're often overwhelmed. Sometimes our intense distress only lasts for a little while, but often enough, it lingers and can make it hard to go on living.

In this book, Sameet Kumar shows how (even without becoming a Buddhist monk) anyone suffering from prolonged grief can use mindfulness practices, combined with techniques from modern scientific psychology, to reengage with life. While many mindfulness practices originally came from Buddhist traditions, they've been adapted over the past couple of decades by Western psychotherapists and researchers to successfully treat a wide range of psychological difficulties. The practices work by counteracting several natural tendencies of the human brain that were well suited to our survival millions of years ago on the African savanna but can make us quite unhappy today.

We humans have a very effective emergency stress-response system that we share with all other mammals. When we sense danger, our heart rate and respiration rate increase, our blood pressure goes up, and our muscles tense, helping us get ready to either fight an enemy or flee from danger. Unlike other mammals, however, we also have a remarkable capacity to think—to review the past and anticipate the future, calculating how to maximize pleasurable experiences and avoid painful ones. In fact, this ability to think was a factor in our survival on the savanna, since we weren't very fast or ferocious. So it's not surprising that when we face danger today, our minds fill with frightened thoughts, imagining what may happen next and struggling to find a way to avoid pain or worse.

When we suffer a loss, this survival system can go into overdrive, disrupting our sleep and concentration and making us feel tense, anxious, or depressed. Our emergency response apparatus is kept on high alert by the upsetting thoughts that pass through our minds as we review past losses and anticipate future pain. Modern scientific research demonstrates that mindfulness practices can help us step out of the stream of thoughts passing through our minds and bring our attention back to what is actually happening in the present moment—the taste of our food, the sensations of the wind, the look of the sky, the feeling of a hug from a friend. By training the mind and brain in this way, we learn to take our negative thoughts more lightly, react to them with less distress, and become more engaged in our lives in the here and now.

Of course, even as we learn to be less trapped in negative thinking, our painful feelings usually don't go away entirely. Practicing mindfulness can also help us deal more effectively with the difficult emotions that still arise. Instead of trying to distract ourselves (which can lead to unfulfilling habits such as watching too much TV, eating excessively, shopping unnecessarily, or abusing drugs or alcohol), we discover how to ride waves of painful emotion, allowing them to come and go. We learn to appreciate that by *being with* rather than resisting our painful feelings, they actually become much easier to bear. In fact, we find that they pass more quickly once we can allow ourselves to feel them more fully.

Mindfulness practices also help us see that not only painful feelings, but all experiences, are constantly changing. As we learn to pay attention to what is happening in the present, we notice that no two moments are alike. Rather, we become aware of a continuous flow of changing events—a sensation in the body, followed by a thought, an emotional reaction to that thought, and then a new experience in the body. We begin to see directly that the contents of our awareness, as well as everything around us, are in constant flux. And as this becomes clearer to us, it becomes easier to come to peace with our losses.

While the journey through grief isn't easy, this book provides a helpful map and guide. Drawing on many years of experience working with people struggling with loss, as well as many years of mindfulness practice, Sameet Kumar will show you a path through your distress. He clearly explains the many forms grief can take and how you can develop a personal mindfulness practice to work with the challenges that arise when dealing with loss. Bit by bit, this book can help you move through your grief and, like the monks I met in Thailand, engage fully in each moment of a rich and meaningful life.

—Ronald D. Siegel, PsyD
    Assistant Clinical Professor of Psychology
    Harvard Medical School
    Author of *The Mindfulness Solution: Everyday Practices for Everyday Problems*

Acknowledgments

What I am teaching here has been made possible by the guidance, inspiration, and instruction of everyone who has taught me so much. To my meditation teachers, loving doorways into the infinite—Sri Das Gupta, Sri Shastriji, Swami Muktananda, Swami Nityananda, Lama Norlha Rinpoche, and His Holiness the Dalai Lama XIV of Tibet—my heartfelt thanks and gratitude. I am also grateful to those who have taught me the art of helping: Ralph Quinn, PhD; Mishael M. Caspi; Jennifer Denning, LMFT; Raoul Birnbaum, PhD; Stephen Levine; Frank Ostaseski; Roshi Joan Halifax; MAPS; and Noel Q. King, PhD. Special thanks to the memory of Peter Goldsmith, PhD, who taught me how to treasure the opportunity to train others to do what we do. You are missed every day.

Thanks to two authors who have been essential forces in my life: Ray Bradbury, who died while I was writing this book, reminding me that it was he who taught me the power of the written word in grown-up books, and Joseph Conrad, for proving you don't have to learn English as a first language to become an author.

A special thanks to my wife and best friend, Christina, and to our two sons, Javier Amrit and Miguel Anand, who have been my guiding lights, support, playdates, and best friends. Many thanks also to our families in south Florida and around the world, for friendship, support, and fun.

I always like to thank the artists who inspire my writing. The list is by no means exhaustive, but those who deserve particular attention are Bob Marley and the Wailers, Alex Grey, Tool, Parliament-Funkadelic, the Grateful Dead, Ustad Nusrat Fateh Ali Khan and Party, Joe Rogan, and Louis C.K. And a very special thanks to Adam Yauch, who sadly also passed away while this was being written.

I would like to thank Christopher McDougall, Scott Jurek, and Rich Roll, whose writings inspired the plant-powered, minimalist running without which this book and my best moods would have been much more elusive. And to Micah True, aka Caballo Blanco, whose spirit continues to inspire me.

And as always, thank you to the staff at New Harbinger Publications for their continued support and trust, and to Jasmine Star for magnificent editing.

Introduction

Even though life is full of suffering, it is also full of the overcoming of it.

—Helen Keller

If you are feeling stuck in the pain of your grief, this book is for you.

The truth is, no matter how close we feel to another person or another being, all of our relationships are temporary. It has always been this way. It will always be this way.

How can we be born with such a vulnerability?

If you look deeper, what we are all born with is the potential to love and be loved. This universal and beautiful truth is at the root of our vulnerability.

The seed of grief is usually love. Without love, you wouldn't suffer so much from the loss of someone you care about. When you think of grief as an extension of love, you might feel a little bit better about your suffering.

But grief can still hurt, and it hurts everyone differently.

Although the transitory nature of relationships is a universal truth, every relationship is different, so each grief is different. Some people seem to fulfill the popular notions of grief. They seem to move on effortlessly, get over it quickly. They may have tried to help you by telling you to do the same.

For you, grief might not feel so easy. For you, grief may seem like being endlessly adrift on a small boat in a massive sea, vulnerable, alone, and without direction. Your feelings may have gotten more intense over time rather than subsiding. You may find that the pain of loss is as intense today as it was many months ago, maybe even years ago. You may feel like you're missing something that other people have or that other people just can't understand what you've experienced. You may feel exhausted, broken, and paralyzed by your feelings.

But what you are feeling isn't unusual, and you're not the only one struggling. Grief has been with us humans since day one, and it takes on many forms. Grief isn't always about death, but the language we use to address grief assumes that. Grief can also follow any massive change to any relationship. Divorce, unemployment, illness, disability, trauma, relocation, migration, and other changes can trigger grief. Prolonged grief has long been part of these experiences for many people. What has changed over time is our scientific understanding of grief and our awareness of tools that can help with grief. Grief has more to offer you than pain and suffering. That is what this book is about.

I wrote this book to help you grow in your grief and to give you tools to help you grow from your grief. As you look back on your life, like me you may find that a lot of your most meaningful growth has emerged from your darkest moments. Times of great change hold great potential, but only if you can harness their energy well.

This book will teach you some of what is known about grief and, more importantly, what you can do about it using current knowledge about how to facilitate ways of healing. I offer a comprehensive approach that will utilize your mind and body to help you feel better.

The first step in this approach is learning mindfulness meditation. The purpose of laying a foundation in regular mindfulness meditation practice is quite simple: mindfulness is one of the most consistent and powerful ways to deal effectively with very intense and turbulent emotions and ruminations. If you aren't able to find a way to tolerate emotional intensity, you may instead distract yourself from your loss with unhelpful ways of coping that lead nowhere.

Mindfulness can help you immensely, and for that reason it is the basis of the approach this book uses. However, mindfulness is something to be careful with if you are intensely depressed. If you find that mindfulness meditation practice makes you feel worse, by all means don't keep doing it. The same goes for any of the exercises in this book. Try everything you possibly can, but use what helps you when you practice it as suggested.

Why do I think this book will help you and why should you believe me?

For two reasons: First and foremost, the techniques I present here are based on research that tells us most people will benefit from them. Second, I have tested this approach on thousands of my patients and have found the techniques to be tremendously helpful, no matter how simple they may sound. For the past several years I've helped people going through cancer adjust to living with their disease until they are in remission. However, the bulk of what I've focused on in my professional life is helping those who don't survive their illness and their grieving loved ones after they have died.

Research by others and my own clinical and personal experience therefore tells me that a mindfulness-based approach to well-being is one of the best ways to cope with prolonged grief. You can expect to feel better if you engage in the practices as described and understand the rationale for doing so.

Ultimately, all of us who work in mental health strive to facilitate resilience in our patients. The word "resilience" might carry a hidden meaning for you that doesn't feel right. It might sound as though being resilient means walking away from your loss as if nothing happened. Part of you knows this is impossible, and you're absolutely right. Your life will never be the same again. Resilience doesn't mean going back; no one can travel back in time, and the nature of life is that it is always changing, always presenting us with different potential trajectories.

For you, one of those trajectories is healing from prolonged grief, and I believe that mindfulness can help.

I recommend reading through the book in the order in which it's written. The first chapter explains what we know about grief and other mood disorders that people tend to suffer from after the loss of a loved one. The rest of the book then presents instructions on mindfulness meditation, along with comprehensive guidance addressing many other areas of life that can benefit from a mindfulness-based approach.

You may already know by now that grief is a full-time job. It fills all the empty spaces you may have in your day and continues late into the night. Your healing also has to be a full-time job. It may seem like the approaches I advocate, such as meditation and exercise, take up a lot of time, but I assure you it is probably less time than that eaten up by the sluggish heaviness of grief and the distracted mind it brings.

Once you start practicing mindfulness meditation, I recommend that you maintain a daily routine around your meditation practice as you continue reading the book. There are charts in this book to help you keep track of your practice. We've made copies of these charts available for download at www.newharbinger.com/27497 in case you need more or are using an electronic version of this book. (See back of book for more information.)

My approach to therapy is to make sure that clients don't need to keep seeing me. This book is no different. Keep the book around as long as you need in order to start a helpful routine that you can maintain on your own. It will help you make informed decisions about what routines can help transform your grief. Once you know these routines, refer back to the book as needed in order to make sure you're doing things properly. But the point is for you to maintain what works for you on your own.

Grief teaches all of us that life is vulnerable, but also that life has tremendous potential. You may grieve the absence of what could have been possible if you hadn't suffered the trauma of your loss, but growth need not be absent from your journey through grief. Let this book guide you as you transform into the best "you" you can be, even if this looks very different than the person you would have liked to be, and even in the absence of your loved one.

CHAPTER 1

• • •

Identifying Your Grief

We are all different. All of our relationships are unique. All of our losses are also unique. Grief will find each of us at some point in our lives, perhaps many times. There is no shame in that. Our feelings are unique, and each of us has different ways of managing our feelings. Just as the relationship you had with your loved one was unique, so too is how you experience the loss of your loved one.

Everyone grieves, but no two people follow the same path in grief. What you are experiencing after your loss is not something anyone has ever experienced before. Every grief is unique. The language we use to talk about grief, such as "getting over it," "getting through it," or "moving on," doesn't feel accurate or appropriate for everyone. Those who find that grief is persistent may feel as though there is something terribly wrong with them—that they are broken, weak, and maybe even unfixable.

Grief unfolds over time. Often, it is not something you move on from, get over, or get past. It has nothing to do with strength or weakness. It slowly becomes part of who you are. Despite what others may have told you, for many people grief is something to figure out how to live with, sometimes for a very long time. Although some people do seem to have an almost innate ability to adapt to extraordinarily difficult circumstances, not all of us can easily deal with the suffering life deals us.

This book is meant to help you figure out how to be healthy on your journey through a grief that feels as though it doesn't have an end. Your grief may feel relentless, a constant intrusion into your daily life. You may feel immobilized by the intense emotions that come up. When grief persists and doesn't seem to be going anywhere, you need to figure out how to deal with it to try to regain some sense of empowerment in your life.

Understanding Grief and Prolonged Grief

You should know that many of us who practice psychotherapy feel that we don't have an adequate vocabulary for or realistic understanding of what you're going through, even though grief has always been part of the human experience. Current researchers are working hard to figure out how to better understand grief, and some of their latest work is highlighted in this book. We have some ideas of how to describe and map the journey. These ideas may fall short, but they are the best that we have to work with at this time, and they are constantly being revised to reflect what people actually experience. However, even though we have some fairly detailed maps of the process of grief, that is not the same as knowing how it feels or how to cope with those feelings. This book will help bridge that gap for you—the gap between being able to describe what we know about the emotional states that accompany grief and how to live with grief.

Prolonged Grief

An experience of grief that persists is called *prolonged grief*. We used to call it "complicated grief," but I think this changed because people realized that grief often isn't simple. Prolonged grief means emotional distress related to the loss of a loved one that persists for longer than six months. For many people, six months doesn't feel prolonged at all. It may feel like just the beginning.

Why does it matter what your type of grief is called? The reason you need to understand how best to classify your grief and how you're feeling and living is because that's how information about how best to help you is organized. Once science has a particular term to accurately describe what people are experiencing, researchers can better identify how to help most people who are feeling that way. They can sort out the most relevant treatments and more confidently recommend which have a good chance of helping you.

Techniques or strategies that work well for one condition may not help a different one as much. For example, if I can fix a car, that doesn't necessarily mean I'm good at fixing an airplane. Just as different types of vehicles may require different types of mechanics, different emotional states sometimes require different solutions.

Stages of Grief

You may have heard about the five stages of grief, a theory pioneered by Elisabeth Kübler-Ross (1969). It stated that people move through five stages in the grief process: denial, anger, bargaining, depression, and acceptance. Kübler-Ross didn't conceive of these as distinct stages; rather, she felt you could move back and forth in between them. However, ultimately the goal was acceptance of the loss.

Although this is a popular theory, I haven't found it to be very accurate for the people I see in therapy. In fact, one study found that it was accurate for some people, but that study only used people who were already coping pretty well and excluded people from participating if they were too distressed by their loss (Maciejewski et al. 2007). Other researchers noticed that the study found that the people who participated in the study tended to have a high degree of acceptance from the beginning, casting further doubt on the value of thinking of grief in these stages (Bonanno and Boerner 2007).

In my experience, the only stages that most of my patients consistently feel are "up" and "down." Those are the only two stages that seem accurate for most people.

Different Diagnoses in Grief

In the mental health field, we organize information about different types of emotional states using a book called the *Diagnostic and Statistical Manual of Mental Disorders (DSM)*. Over the years, this manual has been revised several times to reflect new research and cultural norms. As I write this book, most therapists are using the *DSM-IV-TR*, the revised fourth edition (American Psychiatric Association 2000).

The *DSM* is used primarily to establish categories that help us organize symptoms into clusters that we can connect to particular diagnoses. For instance, if you go to see a therapist, he or she will typically ask you a number of questions about how you've been feeling and if you've been able to do the things you need to get done. The purpose of these questions isn't to shame you or make you feel inadequate; rather, it is to figure out which treatments will work best for you.

These questions can also provide a sense of validation by helping you see that you are not alone in what you're feeling. For example, people who have panic attacks often feel a strong urge to get away from wherever they are. Many people assume that they are alone in having this sensation until someone who is trained in mental health asks them if they ever felt that way. All of a sudden it can feel normal, and you can feel understood instead of ashamed of or frightened by your feelings.

As is the case for many people, grief may be only a part of what you're going through. You may also be suffering from other conditions that affect your mental health and well-being. In the following sections, I'll describe the diagnostic criteria for grief, and also some conditions that commonly afflict people who are experiencing grief. You may or may not have any of the other conditions, but reading through them will help you consider the possibility. Being informed about the nature of your pain is a necessary part of the healing process.

I encourage you to consider the diagnostic categories I'll be sharing with you with the same attitude you'd have when seeing a doctor for the flu. You probably don't feel guilty or ashamed about getting the flu. We all get it sometimes, often through no fault of our own.

You may have been on a crowded airplane during flu season, or maybe you spent too much time around someone who had it. Sometimes there's no obvious reason. You wake up one day feeling a bit under the weather, and it turns into the flu before you know what happened.

Although psychological conditions can't be transmitted like the flu, I think it is helpful to think of receiving a particular diagnosis with the same attitude as if it were the flu. Feeling guilty, angry, ashamed, or stressed about fitting into one or more of these diagnostic criteria definitely won't help you feel better. However, knowing which patterns your feelings are organized around can certainly help you focus on which techniques can help with which symptoms. This is the crucial first step in the journey toward healing prolonged grief, even though you may feel like your journey with grief has already covered a thousand aimless miles.

Bereavement

The *DSM* pays some attention to grief itself in the diagnostic category called *bereavement* (American Psychiatric Association 2000). According to the diagnostic criteria for bereavement, the loss must have occurred within the past two months. If more than two months have passed, then major depression or another diagnosis may be more accurate. Bereavement, therefore, is diagnosed if the loss happened in the past two months and all of the following are true for you:

- ♦ You feel guilty.

- ♦ You think about death frequently.

- ♦ You feel completely worthless.

- ♦ You're having a hard time moving around or feeling motivated.

- ♦ There has been a noticeable and major decline in your ability to work, take care of yourself, or do simple tasks.

- ♦ You see or hear things that are not there.

There are a few important considerations with this category. The first involves guilt. It's considered normal to feel guilty about things you did or didn't do when your loved one died, so the diagnostic criteria doesn't refer to this kind of guilt. Second, it's also considered normal to wish you had died instead of your loved one. This is like survivor's guilt. It's also considered normal to see or hear your loved one, so the last item in the list above refers to seeing or hearing things other than your loved one. One of the most common experiences I hear about is people feeling their loved one sitting or lying on the bed next to them. This is a fairly normal experience and isn't included in the diagnostic criteria.

Now let's look at the time frame. Two months hardly seems like a very long time to grieve an important relationship. For the hundreds of grieving people I've worked with, two months feels like the blink of an eye. Frequently, there's still a lot of bureaucracy to get through two months after someone close to you dies. Changing names on bank accounts, dealing with insurance policies, legal issues, and burial plots—all of these things often take much longer than two months to sort out. This sort of failure to reflect real-life conditions is one of the shortcomings of rigid diagnostic criteria.

Prolonged Grief Disorder

We don't normally think of grief as being prolonged until at least six months after the death of a loved one. The time between the two-month maximum for a diagnosis of bereavement and the six-month mark may be better explained by another mood disorder, such as depression or anxiety. The following criteria for *prolonged grief disorder* have been submitted for consideration in the next revision of the *DSM* (Prigerson et al. 2009).

According to several grief researchers and experts, you may have prolonged grief disorder if six months after the death or loss of a loved one you long for that person daily or to the extent that it is disabling. To fit the criteria, you must also experience at least five of the following symptoms daily or to a disabling degree:

- You feel confused about your role in life or feel a diminished sense of yourself, as if a part of you has died.

- You're having a hard time accepting the loss.

- You try to avoid reminders of the reality of the loss.

- You don't feel like you can trust other people since the loss.

- You feel bitter or angry about the loss.

- You can't do the things you used to do, can't make new friends, or are uninterested in things you used to enjoy.

♦ You feel like you have fewer feelings or as if you're numb.

♦ You feel like life is unfulfilling, meaningless, or empty since the loss.

♦ You feel stunned, dazed, or shocked by the loss.

♦ These feelings get in the way of your daily functioning and are not better explained by a different diagnosis, such as major depressive disorder, generalized anxiety disorder, or post-traumatic stress disorder.

Regarding the last item in that list, these other conditions are fairly common in people suffering from prolonged grief, and all are described below.

Major Depressive Disorder

For many years, it has been recognized that the pain of grief often is tied to what we normally think of as depression. A lot of people think depression is just another way of saying that you're feeling sad. However, feeling sad is only the tip of the iceberg in depression. This condition has a huge overlap with grief, and people with prolonged grief typically also experience depression. In order to be diagnosed with *major depression,* or major depressive disorder, you have to meet the following diagnostic criteria (American Psychiatric Association 2000).

You experience five or more of the following symptoms over a two-week period, including either the first or second symptom:

♦ Your mood is depressed most of the day, most days, and this is noticeable to you or other people.

♦ You've lost interest or pleasure in almost all activities and experience this nearly every day.

♦ Your weight has changed by more than 5 percent (gain or loss), or your appetite has changed such that you're eating much less or a lot more every day.

♦ You sleep too much or too little or wake up frequently at night.

♦ You feel restless or slowed down to the extent that other people notice this.

♦ You feel tired or lack energy most days.

- ◆ You feel worthless or guilty for things you have no control over most days.

- ◆ You have difficulty focusing mentally, more than before.

- ◆ You have recurring thoughts or feelings of not wanting to live.

For a diagnosis of major depression, these symptoms must cause significant distress or hold you back with friends, family, or work or in other important areas of your life. If these symptoms are due to the effects of a drug, medication, or another illness, major depression is not diagnosed. In addition, these symptoms can't be part of what's called a *mixed episode*, meaning a combination of mania and depression most of the day every day for a week. Finally, the symptoms must occur or continue two or more months after the loss of a loved one. If these symptoms occur within two months of a loss, bereavement may be a more accurate diagnosis.

In my clinical experience, major depression frequently accompanies prolonged grief. Mindfulness meditation and mindfulness-based techniques seem to be well suited to treating depression, especially in people who have had it before (Teasdale et al. 2000). I will explore these tools in depth throughout this book.

Post-Traumatic Stress Disorder

Depending on the circumstances of how your loved one died, you may wish to review the criteria for *post-traumatic stress disorder* (PTSD). You might think that PTSD applies only to combat experiences. I've observed that many grieving people whose loved ones died after prolonged or traumatic stays in a hospital fit the diagnostic criteria for PTSD. Particularly intense medical interventions, such as witnessing or experiencing a bone marrow or organ transplant or attempts at resuscitation can result in PTSD for surviving caregivers. Motor vehicle accidents or acts of violence that resulted in severe injury or the death of someone you know can also lead to a diagnosis of PTSD. A diagnosis of PTSD may make it much more likely that people experience prolonged grief.

According to the *DSM* (American Psychiatric Association 2000), you may have PTSD if you experienced, witnessed, or were faced with a situation where you or someone you were near faced actual or near death, injury, or a bodily threat and you reacted with intense fear, helplessness, or horror. While this event sets the stage for potential development of PTSD, the diagnostic criteria include several other categories of symptoms.

First, you must also reexperience this event in one of the following ways:

♦ Images, thoughts, or perceptions of the event replay in your mind.

♦ You have recurring dreams about the event.

♦ You act or feel as though the event is happening again.

♦ You experience intense distress when something reminds you of the event.

♦ You experience a physical reaction when you think about the event or when something you see reminds you of it.

Second, you try to avoid having anything to do with the event by doing three or more of the following things:

♦ You try to avoid thoughts, feelings, or conversations associated with the event.

♦ You try to avoid people, places, or things that make you remember the event.

♦ You can't remember something important about the event.

♦ You've lost interest in or don't participate in important activities.

♦ You feel estranged from or unconnected to others.

♦ You can't feel a normal range of emotions, like you did before.

♦ You feel like you won't live long or be able to meet your life goals.

Finally, you're also more keyed up or on alert more than before, as evidenced by two or more of the following symptoms:

♦ You can't sleep.

♦ You experience more irritability and anger than you used to.

♦ You can't concentrate.

♦ You're always hypervigilant.

♦ You startle easily.

To be diagnosed with PTSD, this cluster of symptoms must persist for more than a month and get in the way of your normal life and activities. To date, there is no gold standard for PTSD treatment. A variety of techniques are used to work with people who have experienced trauma and all seem promising, but none are universally accepted as preferable. The evidence base for using mindfulness meditation and mindfulness-based techniques with PTSD is growing, and the research looks very encouraging (Kearney et al. 2012).

Generalized Anxiety Disorder

Sometimes grief is accompanied by conditions that have anxiety at their core, particularly generalized anxiety disorder and panic disorder. The following criteria are used to diagnose *generalized anxiety disorder* (American Psychiatric Association 2000):

- You experience intense anxiety and worry most days for at least six months about different things (friends, work, money, and so on).

- You can't control the anxiety or worry.

In addition, you must experience three or more of the following, with at least some of these symptoms occurring more days than not during the previous six months:

- You feel restless, keyed up, or on edge.

- You are easily exhausted.

- You can't concentrate, or your mind goes blank when you don't want it to.

- You feel cranky or irritable.

- Your body is tight or tense.

- You aren't sleeping well.

- The focus of your anxiety isn't about having a panic attack, being embarrassed in public, being contaminated by germs, being away from home or close family members, or gaining weight (these are symptoms of other conditions, such as phobias, obsessive-compulsive disorder, or eating disorders). Additionally, the anxiety isn't about having a lot of physical problems or a serious illness, or isn't part of PTSD.

♦ The anxiety, worry, or physical symptoms get in the way of work, friendships, or other important areas of your life.

♦ The symptoms aren't caused by something you take, such as medicine or recreational drugs, aren't caused by an illness, and aren't part of any other *DSM* diagnosis.

Panic Disorder

Another type of anxiety that many people suffer from is *panic disorder*, which is characterized by severe, recurring panic attacks. We all have times when we feel really stressed-out. This doesn't necessarily mean having a panic attack. Mental health practitioners use the following *DSM* criteria to diagnose a panic attack (American Psychiatric Association 2000). A panic attack is a specific period of intense fear or discomfort in which four or more of the following things happen and peak within a ten-minute period:

♦ Pounding or racing heart, or a feeling of the heart skipping beats

♦ Sweating

♦ Trembling or shaking

♦ Feeling like you can't breathe

♦ Feeling like you're choking

♦ Pain or discomfort in the chest

♦ Nausea or stomach pains

♦ Feeling dizzy, like you're going to faint, or unsteady and light-headed

♦ Feeling like you're outside yourself or like things don't seem real

♦ Fearing that you're going crazy or losing control

♦ Fearing that you're going to die

♦ Numbness or tingling sensations

♦ Chills or hot flushes

When some people have panic attacks, they feel an urgent or almost uncontrollable desire to get away from where they are, or at least to know that an easy escape is possible. People who have frequent panic attacks may try to avoid any situation where they're in a crowd, traveling, away from home alone, or even on bridges. When this is only due to concerns about having a panic attack, as opposed to something like obsessive-compulsive disorder or PTSD, it's called *agoraphobia*.

A diagnosis of *panic disorder with agoraphobia* is made if you have the panic attack symptoms described above along with agoraphobia.

A diagnosis of *panic disorder without agoraphobia* is made if you have recurrent panic attacks and, as a result of at least one of the panic attacks, experienced one of the following symptoms for a month or more:

♦ You were continuously concerned about having another panic attack.

♦ You continuously ruminated about the implications of the panic attack, worrying about losing control, having a heart attack, and so on.

♦ Your behavior changed significantly after the panic attack.

Additionally, for a diagnosis of panic disorder without agoraphobia to be made, the panic attacks can't be a result of another psychological condition, such as social phobia, or because of taking a drug or another substance.

When You Should Get Help

Again, my intention in presenting these lists isn't to make you feel worse, but to help you better identify what you're going through. Having a better understanding of your symptoms will help you know what you need to work on. However, if you found that many of the symptoms of one or more of these conditions seemed to apply to you, please consider seeing a qualified mental health professional in addition to using this book.

You should also consider seeking the help of a trained mental health professional if you have limited support. For example, you may not have a lot of opportunity to talk about your feelings or organize your thoughts. A therapist can help you do that. I recommend that you work with someone who has experience in working with grief, trauma, and other end-of-life situations. The type of therapy with the most research supporting it for a wide variety of conditions is *cognitive behavioral therapy*, and that approach is what this book is based on. Cognitive behavioral therapy helps people understand how their thoughts, feelings, and behaviors are related. I believe mindfulness is a crucial part of cognitive behavioral therapy. If you decide to pursue therapy, make sure you choose a therapist who is trained in cognitive behavioral therapy.

You should definitely seek professional help if you're thinking of hurting yourself or someone else. If this is a thought or impulse that seems to dominate your thoughts, I recommend that you get help immediately, before using any of the techniques and practices in this book.

When You Should Consider Medication

Current research suggests that many of the conditions described in this chapter will improve with psychiatric medications. The most commonly used antidepressants, called SSRIs (selective serotonin reuptake inhibitors), are often used for depression, PTSD, and several anxiety disorders.

For a long time, it's been well-known that antidepressants and psychotherapy in combination are often superior to either approach on its own (Cuijpers et al. 2009). However, the benefits may be at least partially influenced by personal preference; in other words, the form of treatment you prefer may be most effective for you, if for no other reason than because you're more likely to comply with the treatment (Kwan, Dimidjian, and Rizvi 2010). A comprehensive review of antidepressant research suggests that SSRIs are most helpful for severe depression (Shelton and Fawcett 2010). *Severe depression* is characterized by uncontrollable crying much of the time, being almost unable to move, and persistent rumination about suicide or death. SSRIs are also used for PTSD, often in combination with antianxiety medications and tranquilizers.

I've found that not everyone needs medication, but if you feel like you may benefit, you should have a conversation with your doctor about which medication may be most appropriate for you. And if your condition is severe enough to warrant medication, I recommend that you also engage in psychotherapy. This book can certainly help, but it might be only a part of what you need to do to help yourself.

If you elect to take medication, take it as prescribed. You should never suddenly stop taking SSRIs without the supervision of a physician. As an aside, psychiatrists and other MDs can prescribe psychiatric medications. In most of the country, psychologists, licensed social workers, and other mental health care professionals cannot prescribe.

Summary

Grief unfolds differently for each of us. The pain of grief may manifest in different ways and is sometimes expressed as an identifiable set of emotional conditions. You can better treat the pain of grief if you identify how it's interfering in your life. If you meet the diagnostic criteria for other mental and emotional conditions, it's important to get appropriate help. If this is the case, this book can be a part of your way forward, but it shouldn't be used as a substitute for personalized, professional guidance.

Now that you have a better understanding of the different types of grief, various conditions that may coexist with grief, and how to get professional help for them, let's explore how mindfulness can help you in your journey with grief.

CHAPTER 2

✦ ✦ ✦

Mindfulness Meditation

The strategies and techniques in this book are well researched. The approach of mindfulness meditation and other mindfulness-based techniques is several thousand years old. Now, modern scientific methods have been applied to researching mindfulness and have corroborated what millions of people have experienced over these past millennia: mindfulness has the power to heal many different kinds of suffering. Mindfulness may not prevent future losses from happening, but it can become a cornerstone of your well-being.

✦ ✦ ✦ practice:
Blue Sky Visualization

Imagine the sun in a clear, blue sky—radiant, life-giving, warm. Now clouds move in on a cold wind, covering the sky in a gray blanket. Above the clouds, the sun continues shining, unconditionally, indifferent to the presence of clouds.

Above the clouds, the sky is still blue.

Notice how you feel when you think of the dark clouds.

Now notice how you feel when you think of the light of the sun shining high above it all.

✦

For many thousands of years, spiritual teachers have taught that part of our minds is like the sun. The mind, however, is also like clouds. Both coexist with each other in the same space. Sometimes your awareness is absorbed by clouds, and you feel down, sad, and frustrated. Your mind doesn't feel like the sun at all. In intense and prolonged grief, it can be difficult to believe that the sun is shining anywhere.

Over the years, many traditions around the world have come up with mental and physical exercises to help our minds feel more centered and identify with the sun rather than only with the clouds. Many of these exercises are what we have come to know as meditation. There are hundreds, if not thousands, of different types of meditation and meditative activities. With the right intention and practice, almost any healthy behavior or action can become a meditation.

✦ ✦ ✦

Origins of Mindfulness

Since the 1970s, a few forms of meditation have been studied extensively by scientists. These days, mindfulness meditation seems to show particular promise, and the evidence base behind its uses is extensive. This particular form of meditation comes to us from the Buddha, who lived in India around 2,500 years ago. However, please don't think you need to be Buddhist to practice this very helpful technique. Thousands of people have benefited from mindfulness meditation practice while observing other religious and spiritual traditions, or even without any religious or spiritual belief.

As you will learn, mindfulness has ancient ties to coping with grief and attempts to wrestle with the big question of why we suffer so much in our lives. You may have an impression of the Buddha as a humble, superspiritual monk who was born enlightened or was in some other way completely different from the type of person that you are. This may make you feel as if you have little in common with him, or with anyone who meditates. However, before the Buddha became a monk, he was a regular person, although very sheltered by a life of privilege. I like to think that if the Buddha were born today, he would be raised in an affluent suburb or elite gated community. He would probably have all the latest gadgets and might even make an appearance in the pages of tabloids, like a celebrity.

At the time of the historical Buddha's birth, a holy man told his father that the boy was destined to become either a powerful ruler or spiritual master. His father wanted his son to become a powerful ruler, so he raised him in a sheltered home away from the ordinary and common sufferings of life. At the age of twenty-nine, the Buddha went on a series of covert outings, sneaking out of the house to see what he was being sheltered from. He was confronted by the realities of life: a sick person, an old person, a corpse, and finally a monk, who seemed to be the most centered.

The sights the Buddha saw, especially the sick and dying, overwhelmed him completely. Nothing in his background had prepared him for any of these harsh realities of human life. He realized that the body he took so much pleasure in was doomed to become wrinkled, maybe even deformed, before succumbing to illness and, ultimately, death. Furthermore, no one was exempt from this fate. All life was made mortal, and all humans were guaranteed a measure of grief on their journeys with other beings.

"Why?" the Buddha asked. Why are loss, aging, and death the universal experience? Why must we all lose those we love and care about? Why will they lose us? Why must we suffer like this? What can we do about it?

Overwhelmed with the sudden knowledge that his pleasurable existence was incredibly precarious, the Buddha resolved to leave behind his sheltered life and become a monk. Ultimately, the Buddha, like Job from the Bible, found that the answers to our suffering are neither easily available nor easily understood. He realized that answers would be available only if he could alter his preconceived notions of pleasure and pain, right and wrong, good and bad. He also found that a great deal of our suffering arises from the mind's tendency to crave.

Understanding Your Grieving Mind

What do we all crave? We crave having control in any way we can over the uncontrollable twists and turns of the life journey. You may avoid the realities of your grief in an attempt to control the pain, but it probably just feels like your suffering gets worse each time you do this. Your mind is trying to control an uncontrollable world—a world that can often feel crushingly indifferent. To do this, your mind, like most people's minds, makes certain key underlying assumptions that run contrary to the nature of our existence.

Craving Control and Permanence

Your mind, like everyone's, craves permanence. Although the world, including all of your relationships, thoughts, and feelings, is in a state of constant change and transformation, your mind is trying to grasp things the way they have been or used to be. Your mind may be resisting changes to the familiarity of your life as it is now, even though your current situation may be very unpleasant. I'm sure you've experienced how hard it can be to try to do something that might make you feel better—your first thought is probably to not do it.

Your grief is a contradiction to the part of your mind that assumes that it's in control or that life is predictable. Your mind is never in full control of reality—none of us are in control of reality. The mind's attempt to control things is always doomed to fail, and grief is the most painful reminder of this hard truth.

The notion that we crave permanence might sound strange to you considering how much pain you must be in and your intention to try to ease that pain, in part by reading this book. Surely the desire for permanence doesn't mean you want to always feel this way! I don't believe it does.

What the desire for permanence does mean is that, even though you may be experiencing emotional pain, your mind finds comfort in the stability of the pain. It doesn't matter all that much to your mind whether you're feeling well or unwell. As with addiction, your mind doesn't want to have to work at trying to figure out what comes next. Pain has become guaranteed, stable, and seemingly permanent. You may find that your mind struggles against participating in some of the exercises in this book. It is much more content to stay put or find something else to do—anything but change, even if that means continued suffering.

Luckily, this assumption of permanence is false. Everything is impermanent, and the circumstances of your grief are the unfortunate proof. But doesn't this mean that the experience of your grief is also impermanent, or at the very least subject to change? There is hope, not just suffering, in the law of impermanence that your mind is struggling to come to terms with.

Intolerance of Empty Space

Part of the mind's assumptions about permanence is the misconception that the future can be predicted, and that if everything in your life is stable, it should always stay that way. Part of what happens in grief, especially prolonged grief, is the stress of confronting a future that's completely unexpected. Where you had plans, ideas, assumptions, and fantasies about what life would hold, now there's a wall of empty space. Even if you saw the loss you suffered coming, the emotional reality probably wasn't something you could imagine.

Now your mind is trying to control this unpredicted and uncertain future. To accomplish this, your mind is constantly telling and retelling a story of your past and trying to predict your future, even if it's a future you can't see. The future you assumed you'd have—a future with your loved one in it—has fallen away. Your mind can't tolerate what feels like empty space where your hopes once were. It fills up this wall of empty space with chatter, rumination, and emotional pain.

In my clinical practice, I've found that for people who are experiencing depression or symptoms of post-traumatic stress in their grief, their mental chatter is dominated by recollections of the past, and it is very difficult for them to see or anticipate the future. If this is your situation, you may be replaying memories of your loved one, such as his or her final moments or days or certain conversations and experiences the two of you shared. This may come at the price of not being able to attend to your day-to-day activities and responsibilities. Rather than confront the uncertainty of the present, your mind finds comfort in the known memories of the past.

For people who suffer more on the anxiety continuum of grief, there is a great deal of mental chatter concerned with uncertainty about the future. If this is your situation, you might also be reminiscing and replaying memories, but you're likely to spend a lot of time worrying about what will become of you. The dominant chatter in your mind might be *How can I possibly go on?* You may also be asking yourself, *How will I meet my obligations and fulfill my responsibilities?* Perhaps your loved one was the primary wage earner or did certain tasks for you, such as paying bills, preparing taxes, doing home repairs, planning social activities, cooking, or cleaning. Your mind may be fixated on your uncertainty about how to do these things, rather than focusing on taking steps to address these tasks. It may find other things to do, rather than working on what needs to be done. This is called *avoidant coping*. I'll address this type of coping extensively throughout the book.

Discovering Mindfulness

When the Buddha realized that everything we experience and cherish is subject to impermanence, his whole world was shaken and he went into a deep malaise. Eventually, his teachings would center on the universal tendency of the mind to crave permanence and its inability to tolerate empty space. But first, the shock he experienced in coming face-to-face with the eventualities he would experience in old age, sickness, and death, along with his anticipatory grief about what was to come, drove him away from his sheltered life and into the company of wild, renunciant ascetics. For several years he wandered in their company, homeless, dressed in found rags, and undergoing increasingly severe austerities to transcend the limitations of his body and mind.

However, despite these efforts he only found himself emaciated, near death, and no more centered or at peace than when he started his journey. He was living on one hemp seed a day when he decided that punishing his body wasn't going to help him address the mystery of suffering.

Cast out of the company of his fellow ascetics for accepting a bowl of rice pudding from a passing maiden, the Buddha journeyed into a forest clearing and sat down to meditate, vowing not to get up until he was dead or had found the answers he was looking for.

We don't know exactly what he did as he sat. What we do know is that afterward he told his followers to practice mindfulness meditation. Over the years, he taught this practice to a variety of people, including kings, queens, peasants, priests, monks, nuns, soldiers, scholars, merchants, and even a serial killer. Those who wanted to ease their suffering were encouraged to test the practice out and see if it worked for them.

This tradition has continued unbroken in several Asian countries. It is now becoming increasingly popular throughout the world. In my own work, I've found that the practice of mindfulness meditation can benefit people experiencing a variety of emotional conditions.

The twenty-first century has dawned with a tremendous amount of scientific validation for the form of meditation the Buddha taught. We don't have to just hope that mindfulness might help us. We can now say with absolute certainty, validated by well-designed research studies with hundreds if not thousands of participants, that mindfulness meditation, when practiced properly, can alleviate depression and ease anxiety (see, for example, Hoffman et al. 2010). However, please note that some of the research suggests the ideal time to learn mindfulness is after an acute depressive episode has passed. Therefore, if you're feeling profoundly depressed, it's probably best to first improve your symptoms of depression in other ways, such as with therapy and possibly medication.

Current research also indicates that the practice of mindfulness meditation can ease mental suffering due to PTSD (Kearney et al. 2012). In addition, mindfulness has been proven tremendously helpful for people suffering from generalized anxiety disorder (Roemer, Orsillo, and Salters-Pedneault 2008).

As discussed in chapter 1, these conditions—major depression, PTSD, and generalized anxiety—frequently co-occur with grief and prolonged grief. Because mindfulness is so effective in alleviating these types of mental and emotional suffering, I believe it holds particular promise in helping you in your grief, and my clinical experience affirms this. Over the years, I've taught mindfulness meditation to hundreds of people experiencing the emotional pain of grief in its many forms. Grief may come from the shock of being diagnosed with a life-threatening illness and saying good-bye to assumptions about enjoying good health and long life. Often grief is about the impending loss of one's own life and having to say good-bye to all relationships. And as in your case, grief may arise from the profound pain of loss of a loved one.

One of the amazing things about mindfulness is that no matter what you're feeling or how grief comes into your life, the practice remains the same. Many of the tools in this book rely on your commitment to beginning and cultivating a daily mindfulness practice. All of the research evidence indicates that people who practice this technique for twenty to forty minutes twice a day experience tremendous improvement in their mental health, and in many cases physical health, after about eight weeks. If you stop practicing after eight weeks, the benefits may persist for far longer (Carlson et al. 2007). However, in my experience, very few people stop practicing mindfulness meditation after they begin to notice how much they're benefiting from it.

At this point in your own journey with grief, you are undoubtedly well acquainted with how stressful grief is, emotionally, physically, mentally, and spiritually. Thankfully, mindfulness seems to be particularly helpful in easing the stress of acutely painful emotions such as grief.

Where Stress Comes From

Your distant ancestor, roaming the savannas of Africa, leaves her cave to forage for plants, fruit, and maybe some bugs with other members of her tribe. It's a beautiful day, and she's hungry. The sky is blue, and there's a gentle breeze in the air. Suddenly, as the wind changes direction, the scent of a lion fills her nose. The scent is strong; the lion is close. She drops everything and, along with the others, runs as fast as she can. Her body is used to having to do this. She's fast on her feet. She arrives at the safety of the cave. In the heart of the cave, which only others in her tribe can reach, she is safe. Finding food will have to wait until another day.

All of our ancestors had to live with these constant threats. As a result, the human body developed to be able to deal with such threats. To this day, the human body is wired to process stress as if it were a physical threat, like being chased by a wild animal. It automatically goes through changes that help it run to safety or fight off an attacker: the fight-or-flight reflex. This is why distressing emotional states feel so stressful. They are all processed in our bodies as if they signal imminent physical danger. The characteristics of the fight-or-flight stress response are probably familiar feelings for you:

- Dry mouth

- Pounding heart

- Nausea, loss of appetite, or diarrhea

- Shortness of breath

- Cold fingers or toes

- Sweating

- Trembling or shaking

- Racing thoughts

These changes all help our bodies run away from danger, into the safety of a cave or up a tree. It's much more efficient to run with empty bowels, so nausea, loss of appetite, or diarrhea frequently accompany stress. It's also much more efficient to run at high speed if you aren't overheated, and sweating and shortness of breath both help with this. In the event that you don't outrun the danger, it's much safer to keep your blood within your torso; that way if you're wounded in an arm or leg, you won't bleed to death. That's why your extremities get cold as your blood flow to your extremities decreases. And if you're stressed-out a lot, there's another symptom you may be familiar with: weight gain. When faced with chronic stress, your body assumes you're in a dangerous environment and don't know where your next meal is coming from. You begin to crave fatty, sugary foods, and your body changes its metabolism to store energy as fat, especially belly fat, to help you survive until you get to a safer environment.

Before you become frustrated with your body, remember that this stress response has kept our species thriving for hundreds of thousands of years. It is our survival instinct. If you experienced a trauma as part of your loss, you are probably keenly aware of your fight-or-flight reflex. Even now, it's trying to keep you alive, but it might be getting in the way of living. Although you don't need any special training to turn it on—it is, after all, instinct—turning it off is another matter.

This is where the steady practice of mindfulness comes in. Although your body will always be wired for survival, over time mindfulness practice can gradually help your body react less intensely and less frequently to emotional distress. I believe that once you do this, your mind will follow. I am often struck by how much easier it is to train our bodies than it is to train our minds.

Mindfulness requires some effort. It requires motivation to want to feel better, or at least to relate to the pain of your loss differently. This doesn't mean ignoring or trivializing your pain. Instead, mindfulness offers you tools to withstand the pain by managing the stress that comes with it.

Basics of Mindfulness Meditation Practice

Diaphragmatic breathing, or belly breathing, is a cornerstone of mindfulness meditation and of many of the practices in this book. This breathing technique is how the body naturally breathes in states of deep relaxation, deep sleep, and endurance exercise, such as distance running. If you've ever been trained to sing or play a wind instrument, you may already know how to do this. Belly breathing is a much more relaxing and efficient way to breathe. In fact, I believe that as the practice of mindfulness meditation grows and becomes part of who you are, you will begin to do belly breathing more and more often, maybe even always.

✦ ✦ ✦ practice:
Belly Breathing

Although belly breathing can come naturally, people under chronic stress usually need to devote some focus to learning how to breathe in this way. For mindfulness practice, you'll eventually be sitting down. However, initially it may be hard for you to get the feeling of how to belly breathe while sitting down, so you may need to practice while lying down to get started. Here are some basic instructions in how to belly breathe.

Maintain good alignment in your spine, keeping it mostly straight but allowing the slight natural curves. Be careful not to arch your back or tense your shoulders. Relax into good posture. If you're lying down, try to maintain a still, well-aligned spine.

Put one hand on your belly and the other on your chest.

Imagine that there's a balloon in your belly. To inhale, inflate the balloon. To exhale, deflate the balloon.

Your belly should rise as you inhale and fall as you exhale.

Practice belly breathing for about five minutes. For most people under chronic stress, belly breathing feels strange if done for too long. It can feel as though you're not getting enough air since you're using totally different muscles to breathe. Your body may need some time to adjust to this breathing technique, which is meant to turn down your stress.

As you practice, notice where your body rises and falls as you breathe by looking at which of your hands is moving. Most of us assume that because our lungs are in our chest, our chest should be doing all the work. This is somewhat true.

Your lungs process air, but it's really the diaphragm, a thin membrane of muscle between your lungs and your belly, that does the work of breathing. You may assume that breathing is automatic, something you do without thinking about it. Although this is certainly true, how you breathe and where in your body the breath originates can have a profound effect on your mood.

✦ ✦ ✦

Benefits of Belly Breathing

When you experience stress, your body automatically tries to deal with it by engaging in the fight-or-flight reflex. Your body prepares itself to run away from the threat as fast as it can because it still assumes any stress you experience is a physical threat, such as an attacking animal. Part of the fight-or-flight response is shallow breathing, only into the chest, with the breaths pumped quickly in and out as you would do if you needed to sprint.

Belly breathing is the opposite of this type of breathing. Because your body automatically does belly breathing when it's relaxed or running long distances at a more leisurely pace, you can trick your body into reducing its stress response simply by changing how it is breathing.

If you're still struggling with belly breathing, don't worry. Keep reading to learn the basic mindfulness meditation practice. With time, your body will probably adapt and begin belly breathing naturally as your practice matures and you get more familiar with it.

✦ ✦ ✦ practice:
Using Cues for Belly Breathing

Once you get comfortable with belly breathing, check in with your breathing throughout the day to make sure you're breathing in this way. I use cues that naturally arise in different parts of my day to make sure I'm belly breathing. For example, whenever I'm getting into an elevator at the hospital where I work, I use it as a reminder to check in with my breath. Likewise, whenever I walk into a patient's room, I always make sure that I'm belly breathing and as relaxed as I can be; otherwise I won't be of much help to the people I'm seeing.

Here is a list of common cues that I've recommended people use to check in with their breathing throughout the day:

- *Waiting at a red light or stop sign*

- *Getting into a car*

- *Walking into your home*

- *Waiting for an elevator*

- *Waiting in line at the grocery store*

♦ *Sitting in a doctor's or dentist's waiting room*

♦ *Entering a place of worship*

If there are other things you do regularly that could serve as cues to check in with your breathing, please write them into the space below to remind you to use them. These can be any ordinary tasks you do, but also things that you find especially stressful or that seem like a waste of time:

♦ _____

♦ _____

Normally, we take these sorts of moments for granted. By using ordinary activities as cues to check in with your breath multiple times a day, you can easily and effectively transform your daily routines, making them much more relaxed and energizing.

♦ ♦ ♦

♦ ♦ ♦ practice:
Mindfulness Meditation

To begin your practice of formal mindfulness meditation, start by finding a quiet place to sit. Make sure your phone, television, and other potentially distracting devices are turned off. Eventually, you'll be able to take your practice anywhere and sustain the evidence-based recommendation of practicing for twenty to forty minutes twice daily. But in the beginning, to get acquainted with the technique and your own unique challenges with it, I recommend a quiet space away from excessive noise or stimulation. Practice this technique as often as you can, perhaps for five minutes at a time, until you feel more comfortable with it.

The following guidelines form the foundation of mindfulness meditation practice:

♦ *Wherever you sit, make sure your knees are below your hips. This will make it easier on your lower back and hips. If you're sitting on a chair or bed, you may wish to use the edge of it so your hips don't sink into the seat. A meditation cushion may help, but it is by no means necessary.*

- *Maintain an erect posture as much as you can, but do so gently. With good posture, your spine should have some slight curves and shouldn't be tense or tight. Gently maintain a dignified posture.*

- *Rest your hands together in your lap. Traditional meditation posture is having your hands resting palms up, one on top of the other, thumbs gently touching.*

- *Gently touch the tip of your tongue to the roof of your mouth.*

- *Keep your eyes focused on an object or on the space an arm's length in front of you. Maintaining your eyes on a fixed location will help align your spine, neck, and head and will also help you realize when your mind is wandering.*

- *Maintain awareness of your breath. I recommend doing this by counting your exhalations. As you exhale the first breath, count silently in your mind "one." With the next exhalation, count silently in your mind "two." With the next breath, count "three," and so on.*

- *Your mind will wander, and you will lose count. This is expected. When it happens, simply bring your attention back to your breath and start over, counting from "one" again. Bringing your mind back to awareness of the breath is, in fact, the essence of mindfulness.*

You might think you're supposed to be able to keep your focus exclusively on the breath. You may even have heard that you're supposed to "empty your mind" or "clear your mind." Don't pay attention to these myths. Mindfulness meditation isn't about having an empty or clear mind; it's about being aware of where your mind is while being aware of your breath. Your mind may not be quiet, clear, or still. Perfect awareness isn't the same as perfect thoughts or even right thoughts. Thoughts are thoughts; feelings are feelings. Be mindful of whatever they are. Notice them unconditionally. Your awareness is like the sun in the sky, and your thoughts and feelings are clouds. Observe them without judgment, unconditionally.

Also, don't expect yourself to be able to practice for twenty minutes right away. Very few people can. I find that, for most people, five minutes is as much as they can do when they start their practice. This is fine. Start with five minutes. Then work your way up to ten minutes. Eventually, you'll get up to twenty minutes, perhaps longer. You can use a clock, alarm clock, timer, or one of the many apps available for smartphones and tablet computers to alert you when time is up.

✦ ✦ ✦

When to Practice

Because of your loss, your life may feel completely disrupted. Your routines may be upended, disorganized, and scattered. When people hear the recommendation to practice mindfulness meditation twice a day, for twenty to forty minutes per session, the typical response is along the lines of "I don't have time for that!" However, I think it's important to recognize that you don't have time for emotional pain, either, but it seems to fit into your schedule. The sorts of things that can help people feel better somehow seem to be much more negotiable than suffering.

On the other hand, you may have an abundance of empty time in your daily schedule. A mindfulness meditation practice can help fill some of this time, as can some of the other practices recommended in this book. If you have too much flexibility in your schedule, a mindfulness practice can help set anchor points for how you organize your time.

Traditionally, it was recommended that meditation be practiced fairly early in the day. This doesn't mean getting up at a ridiculously early hour to practice. Rather, the first session of the day should be in the early part of your schedule, however that may look. Personally, I like to have my first session before I leave for work in the morning. Ideally, this first session should occur before you leave your home, so you can bring some of the effects of your meditation practice into the activities you do during the rest of the day.

The second session should be sometime in the second half of the day. If you do the second session later at night, I recommend not doing it right before bedtime. Chapter 4 includes some instruction in mindfulness-based sleeping techniques, but I don't think these count as a formal meditation session. Doing second sessions just before bedtime is not something that has been tested.

Years ago, I went to a teaching by renowned Tibetan Buddhist teacher Sogyal Rinpoche. He had just written his landmark book *The Tibetan Book of Living and Dying*. When asked a question about scheduling meditation practice, he answered succinctly, "Practice in the morning, and not too late in the day. You need to have waking moments to integrate the practice into."

Tracking Your Practice

For the first few weeks of practice, it may be helpful for you to log your progress in the following charts. Notice if your practice is becoming more organized and structured day by day. The goal is to have a fairly steady and regular practice within a month or so. Because you may wish to continue using these charts in the long term, we've made additional copies available at www.newharbinger.com/27497.

Week 1	Sunday	Monday	Tuesday	Wednesday	Thursday	Friday	Saturday
Time a.m.							
Duration							
Time p.m.							
Duration							

Week 2	Sunday	Monday	Tuesday	Wednesday	Thursday	Friday	Saturday
Time a.m.							
Duration							
Time p.m.							
Duration							

Week 3	Sunday	Monday	Tuesday	Wednesday	Thursday	Friday	Saturday
Time a.m.							
Duration							
Time p.m.							
Duration							

Week 4	Sunday	Monday	Tuesday	Wednesday	Thursday	Friday	Saturday
Time a.m.							
Duration							
Time p.m.							
Duration							

Once you have a stable meditation practice, you may find that you can better organize your day. When I first began my practice, I found that mindfulness meditation seemed to make my use of time more efficient; when I spent twenty minutes meditating, the next several hours flowed more smoothly and easily. I felt sharper and more alert. Still, for several months, whenever I sat down to meditate my mind would tell me that I was merely wasting precious time "doing nothing." However, something was happening: My mind was becoming less inclined to stress, anxiety, and rumination, even while resisting the routine of daily meditation practice.

Although you may feel as though your time is already too tight and you can't accomplish everything you need to do, I think it's helpful to put things in context. For two days, track how much time you spend watching TV, surfing the Internet, and engaging in other time-wasting activities, such as ruminating, repeatedly checking social media, or just sitting around and doing nothing. Here's a chart to help you track this time.

Activity	Total hours day 1	Total hours day 2
Watching TV		
Surfing the Internet		
Other:		
Other:		
Other:		

My intention in helping you focus on how you spend your time isn't to shame you or belittle what you do day to day. Instead, I find it interesting to track empirically how much time we actually spend checking social media, watching television mindlessly, and so on while we continue to resist meditation practice, which can be so helpful. Like many other people, you may appreciate how helpful meditation can be to you in your grief, yet still resist the urge to begin and maintain a regular practice.

You are not alone. Remember, your mind, like countless other minds, craves permanence and cannot tolerate the empty spaces in your daily life, much less in your future. Any sort of meditation or self-care activity at such a raw emotional time as you are going through may be perceived as a threat or danger to the stability of your suffering.

It might sound strange to you: "a threat or danger to the stability of your suffering." However, making changes within a painful situation is often the difficult first step toward healing. Be gentle with yourself.

Difficult Emotions During Mindfulness Practice

If you find that you're experiencing a lot of emotional distress during your mindfulness practice, try to keep doing the belly breathing for a short time. Try to work with the stress of your suffering using breath control alone. If you can get through a few minutes of meditating without crying or feeling intense anxiety, try it for another few minutes a short time later. It may take a while, but eventually you'll be able to stay with mindfulness meditation practice for a longer period of time.

If you can't get through more than a few minutes of practice without feeling like your pain is getting worse, try to focus more on your breath rising and falling from your belly. Does it seem harder to do this when you're feeling emotional pain? Bring your awareness back to your breath as many times as you need to. If the intensity of the emotions continues to be insurmountable, work with the body scan techniques in the next chapter instead. If this is the case, you can use the charts in this chapter to track a regular practice of the body scan instead of sitting practice. However, do this only if you genuinely can't sit through a regular mindfulness meditation session.

Summary

Remember, when your body and mind experience stress, they start to function almost automatically. This is part of what makes mindfulness meditation so helpful. A regular mindfulness practice can help diminish the cascade of automatic stress reactions that accompanies prolonged grief, depression, PTSD, anxiety, and panic.

I would be lying if I said that everyone I teach mindfulness to begins a daily twenty-minute practice right away. It usually takes some time. First, try to work with the belly breathing by itself for a few days. Then try to sit for formal mindfulness meditation sessions. You may be able to do it for only five minutes at a time. That's okay. You have to start somewhere.

After a few weeks, the mindfulness meditation practice will begin to feel like a natural, integral part of your day. I believe that this will happen, and that it will help you feel less stressed in your suffering and more open to some of the positive aspects of the change and impermanence that are inevitable in life.

CHAPTER 3

✦ ✦ ✦

Mindfulness of the Body

The sitting practice of mindfulness is an essential foundation for developing mindfulness skills and cultivating a more wholesome, healthy response to challenges in life. I recommend that everyone who begins practicing mindfulness meditation start with a regular sitting practice, preferably in the earlier part of the day. Once your body is accustomed to regular periods of belly breathing, you may begin to experience some of the benefits of ongoing mindfulness practice in many areas of your life.

In this chapter, we'll turn to mindfulness techniques that focus specifically on relaxing the body. When the first instructions for mindfulness were written down, sitting practice wasn't the only technique that was presented. The Buddha described mindfulness practice as being applicable to walking, standing, and lying down. The common thread for all of these was awareness of where the breath was going and the length of each inhalation and exhalation, and extension of awareness to thoughts, feelings, and sensations and letting them go without judgment or clinging.

The Buddha's instructions were designed for people new to the practice of meditation. Please note that the Buddha did *not* expect practitioners, or even himself, to empty or clear their minds, but simply to observe the kaleidoscope of mental and physical activity. The idea that a clear mind is required for meditation is absolutely incorrect. Eventually, with a lot of practice, most meditators have moments of clarity. However, they don't ever start with them. Please don't be discouraged by being normal—by having a wandering, chattering mind that often feels chaotic and uncentered.

The Mindful Brain

What we know from modern scientific studies of the brain is that it seems to make choices about how to spend energy. Your brain can't easily ruminate and be mindful at that same time, although it will certainly try. What winds up happening at some point during the first eight weeks of a new daily mindfulness meditation practice is that, instead of spending a lot of energy chattering away about anything it can, the brain instead becomes more contemplative about the body. A mindful brain is more centered within the body, and as the attention paid to verbal chatter diminishes, this feels more relaxing and calming (Farb et al. 2007).

Using functional magnetic resonance imaging technology, which can take pictures of the brain as it's working, we know that a couple of months of regular mindfulness meditation changes brain activity from focusing on mental chatter to awareness of the body, resulting in decreased stress activation (Farb et al. 2007). Mindful brains seem to focus more on awareness of the body. If you have a lot of aches and pains or physical discomfort, you may be relieved to know that this heightened physical awareness usually doesn't mean more physical discomfort. Instead, because the stress circuitry isn't as activated, people tend to experience a double benefit of less tension in the body and greater awareness of a less tense body.

Grief Is Stressful

When most people think of grief, they think of sadness or emotional distress. Many of us don't understand how stressful grief can feel. It's fairly common for people who are in prolonged stressful states such as grief or anxiety to have physical discomfort or pain. Stress is inflammatory, meaning that when left untreated, it can cause a buildup of the same substances that cause aches and pains when you have a cold or flu. These substances, called cytokines, are natural defenses that the human body has developed over the ages to help maintain health.

The body still seems to experience almost any form of stress—mental, emotional, spiritual, and so on—as physical stress. It goes into survival mode, assuming that a physical threat is imminent. Your body assumes that it's going to be wounded by an animal or sharp object and prepares to fight off any potential infection. As part of the stress response, your body releases cytokines to temporarily supercharge the immune system. This stress response can save your life if you are indeed wounded or infected. However, with prolonged grief this inflammatory response can make you feel unwell. The stress response system can't be activated at high levels for a long time without becoming impaired or causing problems for your mind and body. The cytokines themselves can make you feel tired, achy, and lethargic, as if you had a cold but without the congestion.

The techniques described in this chapter have helped many of my patients and often have a more immediate effect on reducing stress than sitting practice. However, they should be used together with sitting practice. Most of the research on mindfulness practice has been performed on people who do sitting meditation. You may find the body scans tremendously enjoyable and relaxing, and they are very helpful. But we don't yet know whether they are as powerful as regular sitting practice in changing how the brain works.

Body Scan Techniques

The Buddha didn't have access to functional magnetic resonance imaging technology, but he did realize that mindfulness practice results in greater awareness of the body. He also understood that how our minds behave depends largely on the choices we make in how to direct our mental, emotional, spiritual, and physical resources. Therefore, he taught body scan techniques to help jump-start the process of using our resources intentionally and make it more efficient.

When the Buddha taught body scans, he had some simple advice. He instructed practitioners to review the body beginning at the feet and going up to the scalp and then back down again. These early body scan techniques tended to dwell in minute detail on the "repulsive" parts of the body to help monks and nuns maintain their vows of celibacy.

Over the years, other body scan techniques have been devised. Fortunately for those of us who are neither monks nor nuns, nor under vows of celibacy, these techniques can be quite helpful even without meditating on the "repulsiveness" of the body. As mentioned, a mindful brain seems to become more focused on sensations within the body at the expense of activating stress circuits. One benefit of body scan techniques may be emphasizing and reinforcing this tendency to shift focus to the body.

You should practice body scan techniques in the morning or early afternoon at the latest. If you do them later in the day, they may cause you to fall asleep. The next chapter will provide you with practices that can help you sleep better. But for the purpose of easing your mind and reducing your overall stress level, it's best if you have several hours of waking experience after the body scan to integrate the practice, as with sitting mindfulness practice.

Even if you practice earlier in the day, you may fall asleep doing a body scan. If you do, this tends to be a very restful, intense, and deep sleep. Enjoy it if it happens, but also pay attention to the sleep hygiene guidelines in the next chapter.

As with sitting meditation, regular practice is essential with body scans. My advice is to try each of the techniques in this chapter a few times. After doing so, you may wish to practice just one of them, or you may wish to alternate or combine them. When working with these techniques based on the descriptions in the book, you may find that you're rushing through them or that they are of very short duration. Over time, as you practice them repeatedly, you'll find that it takes longer to complete them. Ideally, each should take ten to fifteen minutes. Don't worry if you take longer. However, if you find that you're doing them in just a few minutes, you may wish to go slower or repeat the practice.

Just as with sitting meditation, body scans need not be done perfectly to be effective. However, as you practice these relaxation techniques regularly, you'll get better and better at them.

Before you start, let me explain the simple stress test that appears at the beginning and end of each of the techniques described in this chapter. It looks like this:

_____

Maximum stress   No stress

Before you start each practice, make a mark along the line (or draw your own scale on a separate sheet of paper) to show where you feel your stress level is. When you complete the practice, you'll find the same test again. Compare your responses to the techniques. You may find that you benefit more from one technique than another. If this happens consistently, you may choose to focus on the more beneficial technique. That's okay. Use what works for you.

You may also decide that each technique serves a different purpose for you. For instance, you may find that progressive muscle relaxation, which involves tensing muscles and then releasing the tension, reduces your stress level dramatically. However, you may find yourself feeling very stressed in a situation where you can't practice it, such as in a public place where it might be awkward to be tensing and relaxing the muscles in your face or other parts of your body. In that case, you may be able to do passive muscle relaxation or a sitting mindfulness practice much more discreetly. By being familiar with many different techniques, you can expand the tools you have available to choose from depending on the situation. The bottom line is to use what works for you when you can.

Remember, though, that even though the body scans are effective relaxation techniques, they haven't been researched to the same degree as sitting mindfulness meditation practice, so we don't yet know whether they are as powerful as sitting meditation or can replace it. We don't know if, by themselves, they can change how the brain works in the same way sitting mindfulness practice can. Future research may very well indicate that this is the case, but for now there isn't enough research to support that claim.

One last note: I strongly recommend that you use the bathroom just before practicing any of the body scan techniques. Relaxation training requires attention to all parts of your body, and you don't want to have to stop in the middle to relieve yourself.

✦ ✦ ✦ practice:
Progressive Muscle Relaxation

One of the first relaxation techniques designed for broad use is called progressive muscle relaxation (PMR). It was invented by physician Edmund Jacobson (1938) in the early twentieth century and has been used with tremendous success by thousands of people suffering from many different physical and psychological ailments. It seems to be particularly useful for people prone to anxiety, panic attacks, and phobias.

PMR is a very simple and effective technique. As you get better at it, you can use the parts of it that you know are particularly helpful for you. The basics of PMR are that when you're stressed, depressed, or anxious, your body tends to be tense. Practicing how to tense and then relax your body part by part can help make relaxation more accessible and attainable in daily life. Your body doesn't need to practice to learn how to be tense, but relaxation may require some training.

Before you begin, ask yourself how tense and stressed you feel. On the line below (or on a scale drawn on a separate piece of paper), mark your current stress level.

Maximum stress   No stress

Find a quiet, comfortable spot to practice. For PMR, you can be sitting or lying down. Standing isn't recommended, especially at first. Do the practice with your eyes closed. You may wish to read over the entire technique first so you don't have to refer to the book repeatedly as you practice. All the counting can be done silently in your mind, as in sitting mindfulness meditation.

1. Begin with your feet. Tense them as tightly as you can. Slowly count to ten as you keep them tense. Then relax, slowly counting to twenty. Notice how relaxed your feet feel.

2. Tense your calves. Slowly count to ten as you keep them tense. Then relax while slowly counting to twenty.

3. Tense your thighs. Slowly count to ten as you keep them tense. Then relax while slowly counting to twenty.

4. Tense your belly. This may mean hardening your abdominal muscles. Slowly count to ten as you keep your belly tensed. Relax while slowly counting to twenty.

5. Tense your buttocks. Slowly count to ten as you keep them tense. Relax while slowly counting to twenty.

6. Tense your chest or breast muscles. Slowly count to ten as you keep the muscles tense. Relax while slowly counting to twenty.

7. Tense your fists as hard as you can. Slowly count to ten as you keep your fists tense. Release and relax while slowly counting to twenty.

8. Tense your forearms. Slowly count to ten as you keep them tense. Relax while slowly counting to twenty.

9. Tense your upper arms, or biceps. Slowly count to ten as you keep them tense. Relax while slowly counting to twenty.

10. Tense your shoulders. Slowly count to ten as you keep them tense. Relax while slowly counting to twenty.

11. Tense your neck. Slowly count to ten as you keep your neck muscles tense. Relax while slowly counting to twenty.

12. Tense your jaw, but try not to grind your teeth as you do this. Slowly count to ten as you keep your jaw tensed. Relax while slowly counting to twenty.

13. Tense your cheeks and lips. Slowly count to ten as you keep them tense. Relax while slowly counting to twenty.

14. Tense your eyes and forehead as if you were frowning. Slowly count to ten as you keep them tense. Relax while slowly counting to twenty.

15. Tense your ears. This may feel like stretching the skin back from the front of your head. Slowly count to ten as you keep them tense. Relax while slowly counting to twenty.

16. If you feel that you haven't experienced enough of an effect, repeat the exercise, starting at the top of your head and working your way back down through the same sequence. Pay close attention to each muscle group along the way on both sides of your body.

17. When you're ready, gently open your eyes. Wiggle your fingers and toes. Gently roll your body over to one side if you are lying down. Get up slowly.

After completing the PMR body scan, mark your stress level on the line below (or on a scale drawn on a separate piece of paper).

_____

Maximum stress   No stress

Your stress may not disappear completely, but any relief will be helpful. Sometimes people who don't notice much benefit from PMR right away begin to do so with repeated practice. As with sitting mindfulness, regular practice increases your skill with PMR, and the benefits.

It may feel strange to deliberately tense and release different parts of your body like this, but part of the benefit of this technique is that it teaches you to consciously control tension in the body, rather than letting it happen only automatically. Even more helpful is being able to consciously and deliberately—mindfully—apply the antidote to tension all over your body, one part at a time, in a healing wave of relaxation.

✦ ✦ ✦

✦ ✦ ✦ practice:
Passive Muscle Relaxation

Passive muscle relaxation is similar to PMR but doesn't include the component of tensing the muscles. Instead, it involves visualizing your body in detail and relaxing each part as you work your way up. This can be particularly helpful if you, like most people who suffer from prolonged grief, tend to have a lot of aches and pains, in addition to muscular tension.

First, ask yourself how tense and stressed you feel. On the line below (or on a scale drawn on a separate piece of paper), mark your current stress level.

_____

Maximum stress   No stress

Find a quiet, comfortable place to practice, and make sure you use the bathroom before beginning. For this practice, it's best to lie down, with your hands at your sides if that's comfortable for you. Again, this practice is done with eyes closed, and you may wish to read over the entire technique first so you don't have to refer to the book repeatedly as you practice.

1. To begin, focus your awareness on your breath. Feel the air enter your body, guided by the rising of your belly. Feel the air being eased out as your belly falls.

2. Do this three times, then close your eyes.

3. Bring to mind a soothing color. It can be white, yellow, blue, or any color that's soothing for you.

4. Imagine that this color is in a ball at the soles of your feet. Spend some time feeling the light from this ball shining in the room. Imagine that this light radiates relaxation and well-being.

5. Imagine this light entering your body through the tips of your toes, feeling your toes relaxing.

6. Imagine the light traveling up into the balls of your feet and radiating down into your heels, and then into your ankles. Imagine your feet being filled with relaxing light, perhaps feeling a bit heavier.

7. Imagine the light traveling through your shins and calves, relaxing your muscles as it goes. Moving slowly upward, imagine the light relaxing your knees, your thighs, up through your groin, and into your hips and your pelvis, relaxing all of the muscles along the way.

8. Imagine this relaxing light beginning to travel up your back, relaxing your spine and then your ribs. Feel the contact between your back and the surface beneath you.

9. Imagine the relaxing light bathing all of the internal organs in your belly, relaxing even deeper as your awareness moves from your bladder and intestines, up through your liver on the right side of your abdomen, and then up through your stomach and kidneys.

10. Imagine this light infusing and relaxing your lungs and growing brighter as you belly breathe.

11. Imagine your heart pumping this relaxing light through every blood vessel in your body.

12. Imagine the light filling and relaxing your chest.

13. Now imagine that the relaxing light enters your body through the tips of your fingers on both hands. Imagine it slowly moving upward through your hands and wrists, relaxing the muscles as it moves. Feel it moving upward, relaxing your forearms and elbows. Imagine it continuing to move upward, relaxing the muscles all the way up to your shoulders.

14. Imagine that the light relaxes your neck and your throat, and then your chin and jaw. Imagine the light relaxing your cheeks, your tongue, and your nose. Feel it infusing and relaxing your eyes and eyelids, then your ears, then your forehead, and finally up through the top of your head.

15. Now imagine that the light has filled your entire body. Feel the light growing more relaxing with each breath. Sense it getting brighter with each breath—each time you inhale, each time you exhale.

16. Now imagine that the light begins to travel down through the top of your head, rejuvenating you, sweeping away all stress and tension, and wiping away any physical discomfort or pain. Imagine that all that is left in the place of any unpleasant physical sensation is relaxation and light.

17. Imagine your head and face being loosened, relaxed, and refreshed as the light moves down; then imagine your neck and shoulders being wiped clean of any tension or stress.

18. Imagine your chest, back, and all the bones and organs of your torso being relaxed, rejuvenated, and refreshed as the light moves down.

19. Feel it loosening and rejuvenating your shoulders, then your upper arms, and then your forearms. Imagine the light slowly moving down into your wrists and then your hands, loosening and rejuvenating them.

20. Imagine the light infusing your hips and pelvis, wiping them clean of any stress and tension.

21. Moving slowly down through your legs, imagine your thighs, your knees, and then your lower legs being relaxed, rejuvenated, and refreshed as the light moves farther down.

22. Imagine your ankles, your heels, and your feet being loosened up, all the way down through your toes.

23. Now imagine that the light goes back into a ball underneath your feet. The light is as bright as the sun. Know that it is there any time you need it. All you need to do to access this wonderful, natural feeling of relaxation is to breathe through your belly, become aware of the light beneath your feet, and feel it infuse your body.

24. Be aware of how your body feels as you rest in this relaxed state.

25. If you feel that you haven't experienced enough of an effect, repeat the exercise. Pay close attention to each muscle group along the way on both sides of your body.

26. When you're ready, gently open your eyes. Wiggle your fingers and toes. Gently roll your body over to one side. Get up slowly.

After completing the passive body scan, mark your stress level on the line below (or on a scale drawn on a separate piece of paper).

Maximum stress   No stress

✦ ✦ ✦

✦ ✦ ✦ practice:
Variations of Body Scans

Several techniques can make body scan practices even more powerful. These are based largely on the passive muscle relaxation technique. Some use specific colors of light, such as white, yellow, or green. Some people feel that different colors of light have different healing properties. If you feel that one color works better for you than others, feel free to use it repeatedly.

The following is a variation of a body scan that uses a healing visualization to restore a sense of relaxed balance in your body.

Before you begin, ask yourself how tense and stressed you feel. On the line below (or on a scale drawn on a separate piece of paper), mark your current stress level.

Maximum stress   No stress

Find a quiet, comfortable place to practice, and make sure you use the bathroom before beginning. For this practice, it's best to lie down, with your hands at your sides if that's comfortable for you. Again, this practice is done with eyes closed, and you may wish to read over the entire technique first so you don't have to refer to the book repeatedly as you practice.

1. To begin, take three deep belly breaths. Close your eyes.

2. Imagine a disk shining beneath your feet. Imagine this disk has the power to heal, to scrape away any tension and stress and leave only relaxation, healing, and well-being behind. It's like a laser beam especially designed to heal your body. You can imagine that as the disk moves up your body, it's like an X-ray that can reveal the inner workings of each part of your body, finding out what's wrong and restoring you back to optimal health.

3. Imagine that the disk illuminates and scans your feet, wiping away any tension or stress. Imagine your feet feeling relaxed and restored to complete health.

4. Imagine the disk scanning through your shins and calves, healing and relaxing your muscles and your bones as it goes.

5. Moving slowly upward, imagine the disk illuminating and healing your knees, your thighs, up through your groin, and into your hips and pelvis, relaxing and healing all of the muscles and bones along the way.

6. Imagine the disk illuminating, healing, and relaxing all of your internal organs, restoring each of them to a state of optimal health and well-being.

7. Imagine this healing disk beginning to travel up your back, illuminating, healing, and relaxing your spine and ribs, and then your lungs and heart.

8. Now imagine that this healing disk illuminates your fingers on both hands. Imagine it slowly moving upward through your hands and wrists, healing all of the muscles, bones, and tendons. Feel it moving upward, healing your forearms and elbows. Imagine it continuing to move upward, healing the muscles and bones all the way up to your shoulders.

9. Next, imagine that the disk heals and relaxes any tension along your neck and throat, and then your chin and jaw. Imagine the disk illuminating your face, healing and relaxing any tension stored in your jaw, cheeks, tongue, and nose. Feel it illuminating, healing, and relaxing your eyes and eyelids, then your ears, then your forehead, and finally up through the top of your head.

10. Now that the disk has scanned your entire body, notice how your body feels lighter, almost weightless, after being illuminated by this healing disk. Sense it getting lighter with each breath—each time you inhale, each time you exhale.

11. Now imagine that the disk begins to travel down through the top of your head, rejuvenating you, sweeping away all stress and tension, and wiping away any physical discomfort or pain. Imagine that all that is left in the place of any unpleasant physical sensation is relaxation and well-being.

12. Imagine your head and face being loosened, relaxed, and refreshed as the disk moves down; then imagine your neck and shoulders being wiped clean of any tension or stress.

13. Imagine your chest, back, and all the bones and organs of your torso being relaxed, rejuvenated, and refreshed as the disk moves down.

14. Feel this healing disk loosening and rejuvenating your shoulders, then your upper arms, and then your forearms. Imagine the disk slowly moving down into your wrists and then your hands, loosening and rejuvenating them.

15. Imagine the disk infusing your hips and pelvis, wiping away any stress and tension.

16. Moving slowly down through your legs, imagining your thighs, your knees, and then your lower legs being relaxed, rejuvenated, and refreshed as the disk moves farther down.

17. Imagine the disk entering your ankles, heels, and feet, all the way down through your toes, loosening and relaxing them.

18. Now imagine that the disk moves under your feet and remains there. It's available whenever you need it. All you need to do is focus on the breath in your body and visualize this amazing healing tool.

19. If you feel that you haven't experienced enough of an effect, repeat the exercise.

20. When you're ready, gently open your eyes and wiggle your fingers and toes. Gently roll your body over to one side and get up slowly.

After completing this body scan, mark your stress level on the line below (or on a scale drawn on a separate piece of paper).

_____

Maximum stress   No stress

Prolonged grief can feel like it's stored in caches throughout your body: your shoulders may be tight, your back sore, your jaw tense, and your digestion troublesome. Body scan techniques may not cure your pain outright, but they can certainly help you relax and develop a sense of healing in regard to your body. These relaxation techniques may feel like tremendous relief in tense parts of your body. If you feel that some parts of your body are much more tense or stressed than others, you can spend extra time focusing on these needy areas.

✦ ✦ ✦

Summary

Body scan techniques can help you tune in to how much stress and tension you've gotten used to carrying around. When you practice body scans, you become more aware of how uncomfortable stress can feel and begin to gravitate toward healing practices that help you develop a sense of relaxation and healing. We know that mindfulness meditation can help increase awareness of the body. When you combine it with body scan techniques, you'll become more sensitive to the messages your body is sending you, which will help you maintain a more stable sense of well-being.

After you've been practicing sitting mindfulness meditation and body scan techniques for some time, you may notice beneficial changes in your sleep quality. This can be enormously helpful for people experiencing prolonged grief. In my experience, most of the people I see as patients who are going through grief have poor-quality sleep. Mindfulness can also be directly applied to sleep and sleep habits. Because restorative sleep is so crucial for healing, the next chapter is devoted to the applications of mindfulness in improving sleep.

CHAPTER 4

✦ ✦ ✦

Sleeping Mindfully

Sleep is healing. Without consistent, restorative sleep, it is very difficult to feel emotionally centered or grounded. One of the most common experiences of people suffering from the stress of grief is a profound and pervasive disturbance in sleep. I see this in my clinical practice often. As exhausting as grief can feel, all too often it is accompanied by bad sleep.

Sleep During Grief

There are many reasons sleep quality is so poor in grief. How well you sleep and where you sleep may be difficult issues for you, especially if you've lost your partner. You may find that you can't fall asleep, that you spend a long time tossing and turning, or that you wake up a lot and can't fall back asleep. You may fall asleep just fine, only to find that you're unintentionally wide awake earlier than you want to be, unable to sleep anymore. You may often begin your day not feeling well rested. Your sleep may be disturbed by bad dreams, a topic I'll address later in this chapter.

Where you sleep may have been affected by your loss. You may not be able to sleep in your bed anymore because it feels empty or the sheets still carry your loved one's scent. You may be choosing to sleep in a room you're not used to or on the sofa. Like many people I've spoken with, you may feel that your loved one is present with you when you're falling asleep, waking up, or dreaming. Quite a few people have mentioned to me that they feel a weight on the bed next to them as they're falling asleep, as if someone just sat down on the bed. When they open their eyes, no one is there, but they can't fall asleep again.

No matter how your sleep has been affected, getting poor-quality sleep night after night can wear you down. Personally, I've found time and again that not getting good-quality sleep makes me feel emotionally vulnerable. I'm sure you've found that not sleeping well is emotionally exhausting and makes even minor annoyances seem like major challenges. Most people find that poor-quality sleep makes them cranky, irritable, and prone to mood swings. You definitely don't need easier access to these types of feelings during your grieving process.

A lot of people who have difficulty sleeping also experience frustration and shame about not sleeping well, especially in the middle of the night. This frustration definitely won't help you sleep better! I think it's much more helpful to acknowledge that your mind is suffering and embrace your mind's distress with the same compassion as you would the distress of a small child or pet, just as you do in mindfulness practice.

Healthy Sleep

Our understanding of sleep has changed over the years. Common thinking used to be that everyone needed at least eight hours of sleep a night, and that getting less would lead to negative consequences. Research on sleep habits has revealed that the situation is a bit more complicated. Let's first get a better understanding of what healthy sleep is. Then you'll have something to work toward it if you aren't already there.

Don't count the number of hours you sleep as the only indicator of the quality of your sleep. The simplest way to determine whether you've slept well is to see how you feel in the morning. If you feel rested when you wake up and throughout the day, you're sleeping well. This is true even if you wake up several times at night.

You may be surprised to learn that the idea that we're supposed to sleep through the night is quite new. For most of the hundreds of thousands of years that our species has existed, we have normally woken up during the night, sometimes for a while, and then gone back to sleep. However, our modern society generally isn't structured for this type of behavior. If you have a job or other responsibilities, such as caring for a child or a pet, chances are the time you wake up in the morning has to be pretty consistent. In that case, being awake for hours in the middle of the night or waking up feeling tired doesn't serve any purpose in your life.

That said, if you can't fall asleep or repeatedly stay awake for much of the night and feel groggy in the morning, you clearly have a sleep problem. If you are awake in bed during the night, you may begin to feel frustrated about not sleeping. Don't look at the clock over and over again. This will only heighten your frustration. Instead, try the Mindful Sleep Induction practice, outlined a bit later in this chapter.

If you find yourself lying awake in bed for more than twenty minutes in the middle of the night, the most helpful thing may actually be to get out of bed instead of being frustrated about being awake. When you do so, you might simply use the bathroom, walk around your home to get a change of scenery, or drink a small amount of water (not so much that you might wake up again because you need to use the bathroom).

If you're going to stay up longer, it's best to engage in a quiet, relaxing activity that will help prepare your body for sleep. Refrain from turning on any bright lights, including the TV or computer screen. This may wake you up too much. Use a flashlight or night light if you need one.

Sleep Conditioning

If you've had trouble sleeping for a while, your body may need to be trained, or retrained, to sleep well again. A lot of people who have issues with sleep use their bed or sleeping area for other activities. Over time, your body learns that the place you're supposed to sleep in isn't really for sleeping. You may then have a very difficult time falling asleep, staying asleep, or falling back asleep once you wake up.

Seemingly minor things like following a regular bedtime routine and changing out of your pajamas after you wake up for the day may sound too simplistic to be effective. However, these are very important behaviors for training your mind and body to achieve healthy sleep. This type of behavioral training is called conditioning, and when applied to sleep, it's called sleep conditioning.

You may have heard about the famous Russian neurologist Ivan Pavlov. About a century ago, he was able to train dogs to salivate to the sound of a bell ringing. All he did was ring a bell whenever the dogs were given meat powder. After some time, the dogs salivated at the sound of the bell, even if they didn't receive any meat powder. Even years afterward, the same tone of the bell would elicit the same response: the dogs would start to salivate at the sound, even in the absence of food.

Conditioning in itself is neutral. You may notice conditioning in various parts of your life, for better or for worse. Certain cues may make you feel a certain way, like suddenly getting hungrier when you sit down in a restaurant. Your mind can become trained to do a variety of things based solely on where you are or what you're seeing, hearing, or even smelling. Here are some examples of how conditioning can be involved in grief, with certain triggers bringing up memories and powerful emotions:

- Hearing a song that was special to your loved one.

- Seeing the hospital or location where your loved one died.

- Smelling perfume similar to the one your loved one wore.

But again, conditioning is neutral, it doesn't have to be painful, or accidental. You can also use conditioning intentionally, just as Pavlov did, harnessing it to help you sleep well once again.

✦ ✦ ✦ practice:
Improving Sleep Hygiene

This exercise will help you use the principles of conditioning to train your mind to sleep better. Just as the mind can be trained, or conditioned, to experience distressing emotions and problematic sleep, it can also be trained, or retrained, for healthier behaviors and rejuvenating sleep.

Healthy sleep habits are called *sleep hygiene*. Over the years, some consistent guidelines about good sleep hygiene have emerged. Read through the following list of good sleep habits and check off the ones that you already do on the left. Check off those you currently aren't doing on the right.

Already do		Need to do
_____	Go to sleep at the same time every night.	_____
_____	Wake up at the same time every morning.	_____
_____	Don't watch TV, read, text, or talk on the phone in bed.	_____
_____	Don't work or use computers, tablets, or smartphones in bed.	_____
_____	If possible, limit activities in the bedroom to sleep or sex.	_____
_____	Avoid caffeine after 3 p.m.	_____
_____	Avoid violent or highly stimulating programs (including news), movies, or video games before bed.	_____
_____	Don't eat within two hours of bedtime unless medically necessary.	_____
_____	Avoid napping in the late afternoon or early evening.	_____
_____	If you need to take a nap during the day, limit it to less than two hours.	_____
_____	Follow a bedtime routine: putting on pajamas, brushing teeth, and so on.	_____
_____	Don't stay in pajamas after you get up in the morning.	_____

As these guidelines indicate, some very simple behaviors can greatly improve the quality of your sleep. Think of your mind as a small child or puppy. Just as small children and puppies need to be trained, your body also needs to be trained to know when and where it is supposed to sleep. This may sound strange to you. After all, sleep is one of the requirements of the body. It isn't something you should have to practice; it's supposed to be automatic. However, from time to time, especially with significant stressors, the body and mind may be so far removed from a healthy balance with sleep that it's necessary to retrain them to sleep well.

All of the suggestions in the list above will train your body to sleep well by clearly letting it know when it's time to wake up and when it's time to sleep. This explains the recommendation that sleeping clothes, such as pajamas, should be used only for sleeping and not worn when you're hanging out at home during the day. Similarly, if you have another space available, don't use your bedroom to work in or to do anything other than sleeping.

Definitely try not to hang out in your bed during the day, and avoid watching TV at bedtime or in the middle of the night if you have sleep problems. I can safely say that most of the people I've seen in my clinical practice who have sleep problems watch TV in bed, sometimes out of habit, but often out of desperation to pass the time until morning. Unfortunately, watching TV in bed usually doesn't lead to a good night's sleep and can even train the body to associate the bed with wakefulness.

If you violate all of these rules but still sleep well and wake up refreshed, don't worry about following the guidelines. They are more important for people who are having trouble sleeping than those who are sleeping well.

✦ ✦ ✦

✦ ✦ ✦ practice:
Mindful Sleep Induction

If you've been having trouble sleeping, the sleep hygiene tips in the previous exercise can be tremendously helpful. However, for a lot of people these techniques may not be enough to help them develop steady, restorative sleep. If you follow all of the guidelines above but still can't sleep, try the following mindful sleep induction technique. It's sort of like counting sheep, but with a mindfulness component built in. It's been very helpful for many of the people I've worked with. Read through this section in its entirety before putting this approach into practice at bedtime:

1. Complete your bedtime routine. Brush your teeth, use the bathroom, and change into your pajamas. Do all the sleep hygiene techniques you need to do to let your body know it's time to sleep.

2. As you lie in the bed, become mindful of your breath. Are you belly breathing? If not, take a few deep breaths centered in your belly.

3. Notice the breath rising and falling in your body.

4. Check in with your body. Notice any tension in your body, especially around your jaw and forehead.

5. As you become aware of any potential areas of tension, bring your mind back to your belly breathing. Try to relax tension as you become aware of it.

6. Bring your awareness to your eyes and your eyelids. Notice them relaxing.

7. Begin counting exhalations, one at a time, as you do in sitting mindfulness meditation. Try to keep the focus on the numbers, letting all other thoughts come and go. If you lose count, remember that it's no big deal. Start over again at one each time you lose count.

8. If your body becomes tense, keep breathing through your belly slowly and steadily as you ease muscles in tight areas of your body.

9. I've observed that most people drift off to sleep before they are able to count one hundred breaths. If you do get to one hundred breaths, simply start counting down, going backward from one hundred to zero.

10. If you get back down to zero and are still awake, go back up to one hundred again.

11. Repeat as often as needed.

Most people are able to fall asleep using this simple mindfulness-based technique. Even for people who have counted a lot of breaths before falling asleep, the night is much more pleasant when they try to maintain awareness of the breath, rather than ruminating and getting lost in thoughts and worry.

You can count your breath as many times as you need. If you wake up frequently and can't fall back asleep easily, you can use this technique every time. You can never overdo it with mindfulness of breathing!

If this mindful sleep induction technique doesn't seem to work for you, try one of the body scan practices in the previous chapter once you've gone through your bedtime routine and are lying in bed.

✦ ✦ ✦

Dreaming

Another component of healthy sleep is the ability to dream. Most people dream several times each night, but some remember their dreams better than others. Like most people, you may assume that if you don't remember your dreams, you don't have any dreams to remember. However, this isn't true. Rather, the parts of your brain that would consolidate your dreams into memory aren't very active. You may just remember fragments of dreams or not remember them at all. Sometimes you may remember a dream later in the day, when you have an experience that reminds you of the dream.

What Happens When You Dream

There are two primary types of sleep. One is called REM sleep, which stands for rapid eye movement. Some people also call this "paradoxical sleep" because the brain is quite active even as the body is sleeping. This is when dreams seem to happen. Your body is immobilized, but your eyes may be moving around rapidly. The other type of sleep is called non-REM sleep. This is when you are completely asleep and not dreaming.

As the course of the night wears on, you go from longer periods of non-REM sleep to more frequent periods of REM sleep. You may wake up right before or right after each interval of REM sleep, since this is the period of sleep when your brain is most active. As your brain is getting ready to dream, the increase in its activity may wake you up. What you experience as "deep sleep," the most restful kind of sleep, is non-REM sleep in the predawn hours. This is also the time when you have the most vivid dreams.

Dreams in Grief

After you lose a loved one, your sleep may also be complicated by the quality of your dreams. You may be bothered by the presence or absence of your loved one from your dreams. In my clinical work, I've noticed that the more intensely people experience grief, the less likely it seems that they will dream about their deceased loved one, especially in the first weeks and months after death. However, everyone is different, and other people may dream about their loved one more easily and more often than you do.

For example, I once worked with Barney, a recent widower whose wife, Donna, died shortly after being diagnosed with advanced lung cancer. For months afterward, he was overwhelmed with distress because he didn't dream about her but their children did. After several months, he finally caught a glimpse of her in a dream. She didn't say anything to him in the dream, but just seeing her again was enough for him.

Be patient with yourself and the dream process. Dreams play a different role in each individual's journey though grief.

If your symptoms are consistent with PTSD or if you witnessed your loved one undergo intense suffering, you may have nightmares related to your experiences. If your loved one died traumatically, you may also be troubled by disturbing dreams that seem to grow out of your loved one's pain. I've occasionally heard stories of haunting dreams where a deceased loved one is in trouble, aggressive, or upset.

We don't know what happens to us after we die. Your beliefs about this may lead you to give certain powers to dreams, seeing them as prophetic or intuitively accurate about an afterlife. This belief may feel very strong when it comes to certain distressing dreams. However, just as we don't know what happens to us after we die, we also don't know exactly what the purposes or meanings of dreams are. We certainly don't know if how we feel about certain distressing dreams has any bearing on reality or if it even should.

In contrast, as Swiss psychologist Carl Jung (1969) pointed out, certain dreams may seem to reach out to you with tremendous power and guidance and feel rejuvenating. These are dreams that often carry life-changing potential, guiding or steering you closer to your life's purpose.

You may have had dreams that later came true or provided you with valuable information you didn't even know you would need. Other dreams may just be your mind decompressing from the day with random events connected to your most intense feelings. When you're in a bad mood, your dreams often extend your mood. When you dream, you may be building events in the dream around a particular feeling or thought.

Your most distressing dreams may just be part of your waking distress, carried over into sleep. You begin to prepare for sleep and dreams the moment you wake up in the morning. Your activities throughout the day become the raw materials for your dreams at night. If you are distressed during the day, chances are your dreams at night will communicate that back to you.

If you are troubled by your dreams, it's only logical that you won't sleep well. All of the concerns about dreams discussed here are normal during grief, and they can definitely affect your sleep quality. They can make dreaming something you wish to avoid and, as a result, literally lose sleep over.

✦ ✦ ✦ practice:

Lucid Dreaming

The Mindful Sleep Induction technique presented earlier in this chapter can help improve the quality of your sleep and may help make dreaming pleasant again. Another technique that many people have found helpful in restoring restfulness to their sleep is using a soothing, repetitive phrase. I've found that if people say simple phrases, timed with steady, rhythmic belly breaths, it can help them fall asleep and wake up feeling more refreshed and restored. It can also improve the quality of their dreams.

Again, the first step is to ensure you're following a good sleep hygiene routine. Once you're in bed, become aware of your breath. Make sure your belly is doing the work of guiding air into and out of your body. Then simply repeat your chosen phrase, saying it silently and gently in your mind once with each breath.

Here are some simple phrases to use. I recommend that you use only one phrase at a time; otherwise you may increase the amount of noise in your head at night:

- ♦ *I am sleeping.*

- ♦ *I am relaxed.*

- ♦ *I am resting.*

- ♦ *Time to sleep.*

- ♦ *I am dreaming.*

When using such phrases, sometimes you may maintain a very subtle level of awareness even after you fall asleep. You may find yourself conscious in the middle of a dream. This is a common experience for people who practice mindfulness in their waking life and use mindfulness-based techniques to fall asleep.

There's nothing wrong with this, but it might feel strange at first. This phenomenon of being alert while dreaming is called *lucid dreaming*. If this happens to you, try to relax into the experience. If it keeps happening, I recommend that while you have conscious awareness in your dreams, you simply stay put and begin meditating within the dream itself. Practice your mindfulness meditation while you are dreaming. This is easier to do if you fall asleep mindfully. I've done this a number of times and find it to be a very relaxing and rejuvenating experience.

Tibetan Buddhists have been practicing lucid dreaming, which they describe as "dream yoga" for centuries. It was taught to them by the skilled Indian yogi Naropa, through his main Tibetan student, Marpa Lotsawa, in India about a thousand years ago. Our understanding of lucid dreaming in the West is relatively new. We owe much of it to Stephen LaBerge and his excellent book *Lucid Dreaming* (2009). If you are interested in lucid dreaming, I highly recommend it.

✦ ✦ ✦

✦ ✦ ✦ practice:
Keeping a Dream Journal

Years ago when I was in college, I had the privilege of working very closely with G. William Domhoff, whose excellent book summarizes much of what we know about dreams (2003). This remarkable man was trained as both a sociologist and a psychologist and has a keen interest in dreams. He taught many of his students the technique of keeping a dream journal to improve sleep and enhance the quality of dreams.

When you dream, your brain usually isn't encoding your dreams into memory. Unless you either write your dreams down or say them out loud immediately, you'll probably forget them within minutes of waking up.

I've found that mindful techniques for getting to sleep, such as counting your breath or repeating a soothing phrase, help people not only sleep better but also remember their dreams better. If you're frustrated by how little of your dreams you remember in the morning, you may wish to start keeping a dream journal. You'll need to keep a notebook and pen at your bedside. A computer won't be as effective. Those seconds and minutes spent turning on a machine or waiting for it to boot up can be crucial for retrieving dream content. When you wake up in the morning, reach over to the notebook and write down any dreams you remember immediately. I don't recommend doing this in the middle of the night, as it will probably make it difficult for you to fall back asleep. What you might find amazing about recalling your dreams in the morning is that you will begin to remember all of your dreams, no matter what time of night you had them.

Keeping a dream journal will help consolidate your dreams into waking memory. Write down your dream or dreams as soon as you wake up, even before you use the bathroom. You can jot down key pieces of information if you don't have time to record your dreams in full. As long as you write something down, you'll be more likely to remember what you dreamed. If you wait too long, you may forget crucial details or even entire dreams. Here are some of the details you might record in your dream journal:

- *What was happening in your dream?*

- *Who was in your dream?*

- *Do you remember any colors in the dream?*

- *What did you do in your dream?*

- *Where did your dream take place?*

- *What were you wearing in your dream?*

- *Was there any music in your dream?*

- *How did you feel in the dream?*

- *How did you feel when you woke up from the dream?*

- *Did your dream seem to have an overall message?*

- *Were you mindful in your dream?*

Structure each entry in your dream journal to address these questions. Keeping track of this information will get easier with practice. As it does, your recollection of your dreams will become more detailed and enriching.

When I've done this in my own life, I've found that over time I begin to notice patterns in what I dreamed about and who was in my dreams. In addition, my recall of dreams became extremely detailed. Whereas the first dreams I jotted down required only a few sentences or a short paragraph, later dreams took up pages.

If you find that your dreams are getting extremely complicated and taking more and more time to write down, you may wish to take a break from keeping your dream journal for a little while. You may find that you have better recall of your dreams in general from this point on because you conditioned yourself to remember your dreams.

If you find that you're getting really obsessed about dreaming, take a step back. The techniques in this book aren't about helping you avoid the realities of your waking life; they're about living more fully while you're awake. That's the purpose of healthy sleep—to give you the emotional and physical energy to tolerate the ups and downs of waking life.

◆ ◆ ◆

Dreams of the Deceased

Many people who are suffering from grief become obsessed with their dreams, specifically with wanting to dream about their deceased loved one. If you are sleeping too much in an attempt to dream more and it's interfering with other goals in your life, you are probably going overboard with your pursuit of dreams. I don't recommend a dream journal for people in this situation; it will only become part of the problem.

Not everyone dreams of deceased loved ones. What I hear from most people who are suffering from prolonged grief is that when their deceased loved ones appear in dreams, they have a fairly passive role. Their loved ones may be present, but like Donna in Barney's dream, they may not be very participatory. Your loved one may only watch from a corner as the rest of the dream unfolds. This is the most common experience I've heard regarding dreams that include the deceased.

I also consider it normal to not have any dreams at all for three to six months after the death of a loved one. Similarly, intense emotional distress seems to get in the way of dreaming about a deceased loved one. Eventually, just about everyone sees their loved one in a dream.

Every once in a while, people have reported having dreams in which they were reunited with their loved one, almost as if the person had never died, or in which their loved one was able to give specific information or express certain feelings he or she had been unable to share before dying. These are the most poignant dreams, because even though you may know you're dreaming, part of you may indulge in the wish-fulfilling fantasy that unfolds around you.

I don't think there's a certain type of dream people are supposed to have during grief. We dream for a number of different reasons, not all of which are understood. The main point about dreams is that you need to have healthy sleep habits that facilitate restful sleep, and being able to have pleasant dreams is a part of healthy sleep.

When to See Your Doctor

In addition to the stress of prolonged grief, a number of medical issues can impair sleep, and you should consult your physician if any are issues for you. In the remainder of this chapter, I'll discuss the most common physical ailments I've seen that can contribute to poor sleep quality. This list is by no means complete; other issues may be present in your life in addition to those discussed below.

Sleep Apnea

Sleep apnea is especially common in people who are overweight or snore very loudly. In sleep apnea, your body stops breathing or breathes insufficiently for several moments at a time repeatedly. You may frequently wake up in a panic because of being deprived of oxygen and then fall back asleep. However, you may not fall back asleep very easily. Sleep apnea can be life threatening. Your doctor can recommend a sleep study to see if you have sleep apnea. If you do, a breathing device can be prescribed to help you.

Hormone Changes

For both men and women, aging and thyroid dysfunction can also disrupt sleep. The thyroid is a gland in your neck. It secretes a variety of hormones that regulate metabolism and energy levels. If you aren't sleeping well, your thyroid function may have changed. Your doctor can test your thyroid function with a simple and commonly used blood test.

If you are a woman in your forties or fifties, you may be experiencing menopause, which entails many changes in your body's hormone levels and the physiological systems those hormones regulate. Women going through menopause often have hot flashes and profuse sweating at night, which can disrupt the sleep cycle.

Gastroesophageal Reflux Disease

If you are overweight or eat immediately before going to sleep, your sleep may be disrupted by gastroesophageal reflux disease (GERD). This is similar to what used to be called heartburn. GERD can cause a sore throat, stuffy nose, or cough, especially in the morning. If your stomach is leaking stomach acid or small food particles into your throat at night, you may wake frequently due to discomfort. Ask your doctor about what kinds of changes in diet or eating might be helpful, or any medications that may ease this condition.

Anemia

If you have anemia, this means your red blood cell count is low. These cells transport oxygen to every cell in your body, giving your body energy. As a result, if you have anemia, you may frequently be tired throughout the day. Despite the fatigue, people who have anemia typically don't sleep very well. Paradoxically, the body simply doesn't have the energy to sleep; it feels like it needs to stay awake to function properly. Since the body isn't getting enough oxygen during the day, it feels anxious at night, despite oxygen requirements being lower during sleep. Your doctor can screen you for anemia with a commonly used blood test and recommend appropriate treatment if necessary.

Medications

Some medications can cause you to sleep too much, while others can cause you to sleep too little. If you're taking medications and have problems with sleep, please check with your doctor or pharmacist to see if any of your medications may be interfering with your sleep. You may benefit equally from a different medication, from taking the same medication at a different time of day, or taking a different dose. However, please don't stop taking any medication suddenly without first consulting your doctor.

Sleeping Pills

If you have trouble falling asleep or staying asleep, or if you don't feel refreshed in the morning, your doctor may have prescribed one of the many sleeping pills currently available. These have become very popular recently, as more people are having trouble sleeping well in our modern world. There are many kinds of medications that help people fall asleep. None of them should ever be combined with alcohol.

If you're considering sleep medications, please be aware that research consistently shows that mindfulness meditation practice has a beneficial effect on sleep quality, and that it also benefits well-being in many other ways (Howell et al. 2010). I've found that many people no longer need sleeping pills once they begin practicing mindfulness meditation and mindfulness-based techniques in their waking life and at bedtime.

If you take sleeping pills every night, you won't be able to stop taking them suddenly, nor should you try to. Many sleeping pills can be habit forming. I've noticed that any pill taken every night specifically for sleep can become habit forming very quickly, even "natural" supplements. Unfortunately, one of the withdrawal effects when you stop taking sleeping pills regularly is insomnia.

If you're taking sleeping pills and wish to stop, talk to your doctor first to find out how to do so safely and if there's anything you should know before you begin the weaning process. You should never discontinue nightly sleeping pills suddenly. The gradual approach that your doctor will recommend, specific to you and the medication you're taking, is much more advisable.

Once you know how to reduce your intake of sleeping pills, use any of the mindfulness-based techniques in this chapter on nights when you don't take sleeping pills. See how that goes over a period of a couple of weeks. Depending on your schedule for phasing out the sleep medication, you may practice these techniques just a few nights a week. However, I believe that once your body and mind relearn how to fall asleep naturally, you will thoroughly enjoy a much more restorative sleep.

Summary

The practice of mindfulness meditation is meant to give you a greater sense of awareness and well-being in your waking life. However, not getting enough sleep, which is so common in prolonged grief, can wear down your emotional and physical reserves. Like stress, sleeping poorly can be physically uncomfortable. The techniques you've learned in this chapter should help you get more healthy, restorative sleep on a regular basis.

Ensuring healthy sleep is a very important way to balance out the fatigue that can come from the chronic stress of prolonged grief. However, it isn't the only thing you can do. In addition to meditation and relaxation techniques, another factor that often enhances the quality of sleep is getting physical activity during the day. Of course, exercise has many other physical, mental, and emotional benefits. Therefore, the next chapter focuses on how to increase your physical activity mindfully.

CHAPTER 5

* * *

Mindfulness in Motion

Restful sleep is a vital component of emotional resilience. Another crucial part of resilience is regular physical activity. Exercise and sleep often go together: regular exercise helps you sleep better, and restful sleep gives you more energy to exercise and do other things you want to do. This chapter will guide you in establishing a mindful exercise routine to help you through your grief.

Exercise and Emotional Pain

Far too often, the most distressing periods of our lives tend to also be the most sedentary. Grief is no different. The silence of your home, the emptiness of rooms that may still be full of your loved one's belongings, and the sheer magnitude of your pain can weigh you down like a ton of bricks. Grief often feels like wearing concrete boots that make each step seem like a monumental task. The pain of loss can feel so overwhelming that we are physically and emotionally paralyzed by its intensity.

Recall cytokines, those substances discussed in chapter 3 that circulate throughout your body during times of prolonged stress and distress. If left to its own devices, your body will pump out industrial doses of these chemicals in response to the stress of grief. Since the body tends to process all the different types of stress you experience as physical danger, you are constantly being mobilized to fight or run away from the stress of grief. Because of this stress response, your body is actually preparing for physical activity, exercise, and movement, even though you probably feel sluggish. Most of us tend to not exercise or get much activity when we're grieving. If this is the case for you, you may have an insufficient level of activity to process the fight-or-flight stress response that's occurring in your body.

A Comprehensive Approach to Well-Being

Meditation is clearly helpful and can be the cornerstone of grief management, but often it isn't enough. In order to successfully manage prolonged grief, you need to address the physical aspect of what you're going through. Although mindfulness meditation techniques can help short-circuit the stress response, I think it's also important to consider what happens to your body when you have so much built-up stress, sometimes on a daily basis. Prolonged stress can be bad for your health, impairing your immune function and causing damage to your blood vessels.

This is where exercise comes in. Exercise should be part of your wellness plan. There is too much scientific evidence in its favor for it not to be. Too often, people who practice mindfulness regularly neglect exercise, despite its importance. Mindfulness, like grief, can easily become a sedentary experience and contribute to a sedentary lifestyle. That's no solution!

With prolonged grief, it can be challenging to start a new routine, including an exercise program. You may feel weighed down by a sense of inertia and seem to be unable to make changes that might ease your pain. The hardest part of changing behaviors is often the beginning, when you're trying to start doing things differently. As the Chinese Taoist master Lao-tzu said, "The journey of a thousand miles begins with a single step." You have to find an active way to mobilize change in your grief and in your life.

Having to make a deliberate and mindful attempt to incorporate physical activity into our routines is very new for our species. For millennia, human beings had no choice but to live extremely active lives. Until very recently, daily survival required long walks, hunting, running, plowing fields, herding animals, or manual labor for almost everyone. Even today, in much of the world survival still requires putting in hours of physical work daily. You won't find gyms in areas where people have to work outside in the hot sun for hours every day to put food on the table; they simply aren't needed.

But like many people in the developed world, you may live a fairly sedentary life. For most of us, especially as we age, including physical activity in our routines requires planning and discipline. Especially when experiencing intense grief, you may need to make a conscious effort to just change out of your pajamas, bathe, or brush your teeth every day. Pumped full of unused cytokines due to the stress of grief, your body probably feels sluggish, lethargic, and unmotivated.

Yet this is all the more reason to explore every technique at your disposal to feel better. Science has proven that physical activity plays a crucial role in emotional well-being. This isn't to say that those who have to toil in fields or mines feel better because of working under difficult conditions. However, what we do know is that without some sort of physical activity, our minds don't do as well. Whereas in some societies a grueling level of activity is required, our society is generally at the other extreme, resulting in an unprecedented level of inactivity.

Like most people in our society, you may assume that any talk of exercise is also about weight loss. Most ads for gyms or exercise equipment make claims about how many pounds you can lose using their system. This chapter isn't about weight loss, although you may find that exercise helps you maintain a more stable and healthful weight. What I want you to focus on as you read about exercise is the effects that physical activity can have on your mood. I'd like you to think of starting an exercise routine as part of a path to emotional health—something that numbers on a weight scale can't accurately measure.

Research on Exercise and Depression

A lot of approaches to grief neglect the importance of exercise. This is unfortunate because we're constantly learning about how important exercise is for all of us. Researchers are consistently finding that exercise can be *neuroprotective*, meaning exercise can help protect the brain from the effects of aging and distressing mood states (see Kramer et al. 2005 for a review).

In addition, studies indicate that exercising regularly in sufficient doses can be as powerful as an antidepressant medication such as sertraline, also known as Zoloft (Blumenthal et al. 1999, 2007). For example, in a 2007 study (Blumenthal et al. 2007), 202 people diagnosed with major depression were divided into four groups. One group was put on the antidepressant sertraline without any exercise, one group was given a placebo drug without exercise, one group did exercise under supervision without the drug, and the final group did unsupervised exercise at home, also without the drug.

At the end of sixteen weeks, the researchers found that all the groups except the one receiving a placebo drug had similar reductions in depression. The group that took antidepressant medication had a faster decline in depression scores, but their final scores didn't differ significantly from the improvement reported by the two groups that exercised after about four months. This means that exercise may take a little longer to reduce depression, but in the long run it can be as effective as some medications.

It's also worthwhile to keep in mind that the groups that exercised didn't have to deal with the side effects of the medication. Although the researchers didn't measure all possible side effects, it would be interesting to look at whether the groups that exercised tended to sleep better and what kinds of changes in weight and libido they might have experienced in comparison to the group taking medication.

If you're taking sertraline or another antidepressant, please don't interpret the results of this study to mean you can stop taking your medication if you exercise. Please check with your prescribing doctor first. These kinds of medications can't be stopped suddenly; they must be tapered off under a doctor's supervision. Furthermore, you should never make any changes in psychiatric medications unless you're making healthy changes in your lifestyle.

Choosing the Right Exercise for You

There are many different forms of exercise to choose from. Some of the most popular are cardiovascular training (like running or bicycling), weight bearing, and dance (like Zumba or line dancing). Any of these can help you manage your mood. If you have cardiovascular issues or an injury, you may benefit more from gentler, low-impact exercise, such as yoga or tai chi. If you play sports, you can certainly include that as a form of exercise if you get an aerobic workout during practices and games.

If you haven't been exercising for a long time or haven't ever had a regular exercise program, be sure to consult your physician to make sure you're healthy enough to begin. You may need a cardiac stress test just to make sure you can handle whatever form of exercise you choose to do, even if it isn't in the cardiovascular category. Any type of exercise will increase your heart rate. If you plan on running or doing another form of exercise that places high demands on your cardiovascular system, it's especially important to make sure your heart is healthy enough first.

If you're overweight or obese or haven't exercised in a long time, choose a gentle method of exercise, such as walking or water aerobics (exercising in a shallow pool), to begin with. People who are overweight or out of shape and suddenly decide to start running or lifting weights can easily do unintended damage to their joints or tissues or throw their back out. This won't help your emotional state.

Start easy and gently. Be as patient with your body as meditation has taught you to be with your mind. Take your time to get into better physical shape. Just as with meditation, small steps can lead to big changes.

Exercise and Mindfulness: Old Friends

Although I feel like it's neglected, the relationship between mindfulness and physical activity isn't new. Historically, Buddhist monks who practiced mindfulness also begged for their food. This frequently entailed walking from where they slept, often far outside of villages or towns, with a begging bowl and walking stick. They would go from house to house until they had enough food—often unrefrigerated leftovers from the previous day—and then walk back to their sleeping quarters. These early monks had to walk for miles to obtain food, in addition to practicing meditation for hours. Physical activity was part of their practice. They didn't need a gym, and their intensive meditation practice didn't mean having a sedentary lifestyle—they walked everywhere, for hours each day.

Cultures influenced by Buddhism or with preexisting traditions of regular meditation practice have long recognized the importance of physical exercise. In India, meditators have also practiced hatha yoga, which has become immensely popular around the world. Hatha yoga involves a series of mindful physical movements, often timed with the breath, that help relax the body and make practitioners aware of their movements.

In China and Japan, martial arts based on circulating the vital energies of the body have been practiced by monks and laypeople who meditate regularly. Like yoga, martial arts such as tai chi, kung fu, and aikido stretch and invigorate the practitioner's body. They are energetic complements to an otherwise sedentary meditation practice.

✦ ✦ ✦ practice:
Moving Meditation

During lengthy meditation sessions, such as full-day retreats, periods of sitting meditation are often interspersed with walking meditation. To practice walking meditation on your own, find a spacious place to practice. Walking meditation can be done indoors or outdoors, weather permitting. Make sure you have enough space to walk around in.

Begin by doing sitting mindfulness meditation for at least ten minutes. When you're ready to transition to walking meditation, stand up slowly while exhaling. Take a deep breath into your belly once you're standing, then release it. Feel your feet grounded firmly and evenly on the floor or earth. Standing this way, take another belly breath and exhale slowly as you feel your body connecting with the ground through your feet.

As you inhale, slowly raise your right heel. Shift your weight to your left foot. As you exhale, bring your right heel down on the ground in a step in front of you and slowly raise your left heel.

As you inhale, raise your left foot completely off the ground as you begin to step. Pause midstep, with your left foot in the air in midstride, balancing on your right foot. Do this for however long you can. While exhaling, bring your left foot down heel first to complete the step.

As your left heel touches the ground, lift your right heel, shifting your weight back to your left foot. Again, pause midstep, with your right foot in the air midstride, and balance on your left foot for as long as you can. While exhaling, bring your right food down heel first to complete the step.

Repeat this for twenty-one breaths, stopping midstride in each step. This number of breaths has traditionally been used for meditation practices in the Tibetan tradition with which I am most familiar, and it seems to work well for most people. However, you can extend the practice for as long as you wish. Walking meditation is typically done in a circle with other practitioners. You can also walk mindfully in a circle by yourself. If you're practicing with a group, try to time your steps and your breath together.

Once you've developed this kind of mindfulness in motion with walking, you can apply it to any form of exercise you choose. I like to run, and I often count my exhalations as a way of transforming running into a meditation. You can count your breaths while on a treadmill, walking regularly, or swimming. I've also found mindfulness of my posture during exercise to be invaluable; it's probably saved me from many injuries. Additionally, breathing mindfully through the belly can give you added endurance during many kinds of exercise.

✦ ✦ ✦

Making a Commitment

In my opinion, you shouldn't learn yoga or martial arts from a book. You should seek out a school that can put you in touch with an instructor who can offer you guidance and correct your posture as you engage in these practices.

If you enroll in a class to learn these techniques, you'll also reap the benefit of spending less time alone. Instead, you'll be with a group of people who are all interested in the same thing. Another benefit of taking classes is that signing up creates a financial and social commitment. If you're the type of person who needs to sign up and pay to do something to help motivate yourself, signing up for classes at a yoga studio or martial arts dojo can help you do that.

Staying on Track

One of the main complaints I've heard from people is that they feel like mindfulness and exercise aren't helping them as much as they'd hoped or expected. On closer examination, this is almost always because they weren't practicing for the recommended amounts of time.

With these kinds of practices, it's helpful to think of the amount of time you do them as a dosage. Imagine that you have a really bad headache. Would half an aspirin help? Would you take half an ibuprofen if you had a broken bone? If you did, you could say the medicine wasn't helpful for you. However, the problem wasn't the form of treatment; it was the dose. It's the same with mindfulness and exercise.

In this chapter, I've included charts for you to fill out to document your practice of both mindfulness meditation and exercise each week. You'll find sixteen weekly tracking charts, because that's the recommended minimum duration of an exercise program to promote well-being. You may wish to continue using these charts after the sixteen weeks have passed; you can find blank versions to download at www.newharbinger.com/27497.

As previously mentioned, the dose for mindfulness is two twenty- to forty-minute sessions daily, ideally for at least eight weeks, and longer if you'd like. Most people take some time to work their way up to twenty to forty minutes of meditation. For many people, sixteen weeks is a sufficient period of time within which to build up their practice and then sustain eight weeks of consistent mindfulness practice at the recommended level. If you're able to start with the recommended doses of mindfulness meditation right away, you might still wish to continue your practice for at least sixteen weeks. In my experience, most people find mindfulness meditation quite restorative and healing and continue to practice long after the prescribed time period ends.

The dosage for exercise in terms of maintaining well-being is twenty to thirty minutes at least three times a week for sixteen weeks. You can certainly do more if you'd like, but not less. I've included two slots for exercise in the charts in case you choose to do different types of exercise. For example, if you'd like to use a treadmill a couple of days per week and go to a yoga class on other days, you can mark your treadmill workout as Exercise 1, and yoga as Exercise 2.

You'll also find a stress assessment like the one that appeared with the body scans before the chart for each week, along with a similar scale for energy level. At the start of each week, mark where you feel your stress level and energy level are in general, meaning how stressed and how energetic you feel most of the day. It's fine to make a rough guess about each of these; don't worry about getting it exactly right.

Before the week 1 chart, after the week 8 chart, and again after the last chart, you'll find a similar well-being scale. Make a mark along the line to indicate your overall sense of well-being. You can use all three scales to help you see whether you're moving in the direction you'd like. If there isn't as much change as you'd hoped, please keep trying. The rate of improvement can vary based on many factors, including individual differences between people.

Initial Assessment

Make a mark on each line to indicate roughly where you are on this continuum.

_____

Maximum stress   No stress

_____

No energy   Maximum energy

_____

No well-being   Maximum well-being

Comments:

_____

_____

_____

_____

_____

_____

_____

_____

Meditation and Exercise Tracking Chart

Week 1	Sunday	Monday	Tuesday	Wednesday	Thursday	Friday	Saturday
Mindfulness Session 1							
Mindfulness Session 2							
Exercise 1							
Exercise 2							

Week 2 Assessment

Make a mark on each line to indicate roughly where you are on this continuum.

_____

Maximum stress   No stress

_____

No energy   Maximum energy

Comments:

_____

_____

_____

_____

_____

_____

_____

_____

_____

_____

Meditation and Exercise Tracking Chart

Week 2	Sunday	Monday	Tuesday	Wednesday	Thursday	Friday	Saturday
Mindfulness Session 1							
Mindfulness Session 2							
Exercise 1							
Exercise 2							

Week 3 Assessment

Make a mark on each line to indicate roughly where you are on this continuum.

_____

Maximum stress   No stress

_____

No energy   Maximum energy

Comments:

_____

_____

_____

_____

_____

_____

_____

_____

Meditation and Exercise Tracking Chart

Week 3	Sunday	Monday	Tuesday	Wednesday	Thursday	Friday	Saturday
Mindfulness Session 1							
Mindfulness Session 2							
Exercise 1							
Exercise 2							

Week 4 Assessment

Make a mark on each line to indicate roughly where you are on this continuum.

_____

Maximum stress   No stress

_____

No energy   Maximum energy

Comments:

_____

_____

_____

_____

_____

_____

_____

_____

_____

Meditation and Exercise Tracking Chart

Week 4	Sunday	Monday	Tuesday	Wednesday	Thursday	Friday	Saturday
Mindfulness Session 1							
Mindfulness Session 2							
Exercise 1							
Exercise 2							

Week 5 Assessment

Make a mark on each line to indicate roughly where you are on this continuum.

_____

Maximum stress   No stress

_____

No energy   Maximum energy

Comments:

_____

_____

_____

_____

_____

_____

_____

_____

_____

Meditation and Exercise Tracking Chart

Week 5	Sunday	Monday	Tuesday	Wednesday	Thursday	Friday	Saturday
Mindfulness Session 1							
Mindfulness Session 2							
Exercise 1							
Exercise 2							

Week 6 Assessment

Make a mark on each line to indicate roughly where you are on this continuum.

_____

Maximum stress   No stress

_____

No energy   Maximum energy

Comments:

_____

_____

_____

_____

_____

_____

_____

_____

_____

_____

Meditation and Exercise Tracking Chart

Week 6	Sunday	Monday	Tuesday	Wednesday	Thursday	Friday	Saturday
Mindfulness Session 1							
Mindfulness Session 2							
Exercise 1							
Exercise 2							

Week 7 Assessment

Make a mark on each line to indicate roughly where you are on this continuum.

_____

Maximum stress   No stress

_____

No energy   Maximum energy

Comments:

_____

_____

_____

_____

_____

_____

_____

_____

_____

Meditation and Exercise Tracking Chart

Week 7	Sunday	Monday	Tuesday	Wednesday	Thursday	Friday	Saturday
Mindfulness Session 1							
Mindfulness Session 2							
Exercise 1							
Exercise 2							

Week 8 Assessment

Make a mark on each line to indicate roughly where you are on this continuum.

_____

Maximum stress   No stress

_____

No energy   Maximum energy

Comments:

_____

_____

_____

_____

_____

_____

_____

Midpoint Well-Being Assessment

_____

No well-being   Maximum well-being

Meditation and Exercise Tracking Chart

Week 8	Sunday	Monday	Tuesday	Wednesday	Thursday	Friday	Saturday
Mindfulness Session 1							
Mindfulness Session 2							
Exercise 1							
Exercise 2							

Week 9 Assessment

Make a mark on each line to indicate roughly where you are on this continuum.

_____

Maximum stress   No stress

_____

No energy   Maximum energy

Comments:

_____

_____

_____

_____

_____

_____

_____

_____

_____

Meditation and Exercise Tracking Chart

Week 9	Sunday	Monday	Tuesday	Wednesday	Thursday	Friday	Saturday
Mindfulness Session 1							
Mindfulness Session 2							
Exercise 1							
Exercise 2							

Week 10 Assessment

Make a mark on each line to indicate roughly where you are on this continuum.

_____

Maximum stress   No stress

_____

No energy   Maximum energy

Comments:

_____

_____

_____

_____

_____

_____

_____

_____

_____

Meditation and Exercise Tracking Chart

Week 10	Sunday	Monday	Tuesday	Wednesday	Thursday	Friday	Saturday
Mindfulness Session 1							
Mindfulness Session 2							
Exercise 1							
Exercise 2							

Week 11 Assessment

Make a mark on each line to indicate roughly where you are on this continuum.

_____

Maximum stress   No stress

_____

No energy   Maximum energy

Comments:

_____

_____

_____

_____

_____

_____

_____

_____

_____

_____

Meditation and Exercise Tracking Chart

Week 11	Sunday	Monday	Tuesday	Wednesday	Thursday	Friday	Saturday
Mindfulness Session 1							
Mindfulness Session 2							
Exercise 1							
Exercise 2							

Week 12 Assessment

Make a mark on each line to indicate roughly where you are on this continuum.

_____

Maximum stress   No stress

_____

No energy   Maximum energy

Comments:

_____

_____

_____

_____

_____

_____

_____

_____

_____

Meditation and Exercise Tracking Chart

Week 12	Sunday	Monday	Tuesday	Wednesday	Thursday	Friday	Saturday
Mindfulness Session 1							
Mindfulness Session 2							
Exercise 1							
Exercise 2							

Week 13 Assessment

Make a mark on each line to indicate roughly where you are on this continuum.

_____

Maximum stress   No stress

_____

No energy   Maximum energy

Comments:

_____

_____

_____

_____

_____

_____

_____

_____

_____

Meditation and Exercise Tracking Chart

Week 13	Sunday	Monday	Tuesday	Wednesday	Thursday	Friday	Saturday
Mindfulness Session 1							
Mindfulness Session 2							
Exercise 1							
Exercise 2							

Week 14 Assessment

Make a mark on each line to indicate roughly where you are on this continuum.

_____

Maximum stress   No stress

_____

No energy   Maximum energy

Comments:

_____

_____

_____

_____

_____

_____

_____

_____

_____

_____

Meditation and Exercise Tracking Chart

Week 14	Sunday	Monday	Tuesday	Wednesday	Thursday	Friday	Saturday
Mindfulness Session 1							
Mindfulness Session 2							
Exercise 1							
Exercise 2							

Week 15 Assessment

Make a mark on each line to indicate roughly where you are on this continuum.

_____

Maximum stress   No stress

_____

No energy   Maximum energy

Comments:

_____

_____

_____

_____

_____

_____

_____

_____

_____

Meditation and Exercise Tracking Chart

Week 15	Sunday	Monday	Tuesday	Wednesday	Thursday	Friday	Saturday
Mindfulness Session 1							
Mindfulness Session 2							
Exercise 1							
Exercise 2							

Week 16 Assessment

Make a mark on each line to indicate roughly where you are on this continuum.

_____

Maximum stress   No stress

_____

No energy   Maximum energy

Comments:

_____

_____

_____

_____

_____

_____

_____

_____

_____

_____

Meditation and Exercise Tracking Chart

Week 16	Sunday	Monday	Tuesday	Wednesday	Thursday	Friday	Saturday
Mindfulness Session 1							
Mindfulness Session 2							
Exercise 1							
Exercise 2							

Final Assessment

| Maximum stress | No stress |

| No energy | Maximum energy |

| No well-being | Maximum well-being |

Mindfulness and Your Body

Research using brain scans has shown that mindfulness meditation can increase the amount of energy the brain devotes to being aware of the body while diminishing thoughts and feelings associated with depression (Farb et al. 2007). Mindfulness can help you feel more in touch with pleasant sensations in your body and thereby help your mind feel less distress.

From what this research on mindfulness and the brain reveals, choices you make about how to spend your time can have a profound impact on your mood by literally rewiring your brain. Mindfulness meditation and exercise both seem to increase the brain's awareness of the body. People who study the brain call this body-centered awareness *somatosensory awareness*. In general, the more somatosensory awareness your brain has as a result of behavioral choices, the less likely it is to focus its energy on distressing mental chatter.

When you begin meditating and exercising regularly, you get more in touch with many different aspects of physical health while also reducing the intensity of your stress response. As mentioned previously, becoming more aware of your body through meditation doesn't mean focusing more on pain or feeling achy. Instead, what seems to happen in the brain as people's meditation practice and exercise routines crystallize over several weeks is that they have an increased ability to experience emotional states as *temporary* physical sensations. This is quite different from feeling as though your emotional pain or physical symptoms will never go away.

For example, before starting a daily meditation routine, you may have often felt extremely anxious. At such times, your breath became rapid and shallow, your mind raced, and you may have felt completely overwhelmed. When you have a regular meditation practice, you may still get anxious. However, you're also likely to more easily notice that your breathing has changed and be able to intentionally shift it back to a more relaxed pattern, such as belly breathing. In addition, you're likely to more easily notice that your body is tense in certain spots and be able to intentionally adjust your posture or relax those parts of your body. The anxiety still happens, but because you experience it differently, you can deal with it differently. The feeling doesn't automatically take over your mind, engulf you, and ruin your day. Most importantly, your mental chatter doesn't feed into a sense of overwhelmed helplessness.

Summary

Grief can feel like something too powerful and immense that's happening to you. You can feel like you're a helpless victim of its crushing emotions. Implementing changes such as regularly engaging in mindfulness meditation and exercise transforms your grief into a process in which you're actively involved, rather than something that's being inflicted on you. You're becoming an active participant again in the choices you're making, and beginning to transition from victim to survivor.

Exercise can help you get more in touch with the active role you still have in creating and re-creating your life after your loss. It's also an important way to take care of yourself at any time, but especially in difficult times. The reluctance to take care of yourself that shows up as not exercising can also manifest in other areas of your life, including eating well. Therefore, the next chapter explores how you can nourish yourself mindfully, expanding and deepening your mindfulness practice in the process.

CHAPTER 6

+ + +

Mindful Sustenance

The emotional burden of grief can make it tricky to start and maintain an exercise routine. Hopefully, the previous chapter has helped you with that, and by now you're starting to feel the emotional and physical benefits of regular exercise. Although you may not be feeling happy all the time (which isn't a realistic goal for anyone), you may have a bit less distress or find that your distress isn't as intense or doesn't occur as often. You may feel that some of the intense sharpness of your pain is beginning to dull. This will be an ongoing and gradual process. Grief isn't like a footrace with a finish line at the end. Sometimes it just fades in intensity over what can feel like an eternity as it becomes part of who you are.

Physical activity has long been linked with emotional health and well-being. Mindfulness meditation and exercise as part of your daily routines can be incredibly helpful in boosting your ability to feel better. Even if the gains sometimes last only a few moments, those are moments better spent with healing and nurturing feelings rather than with the difficult emotions of prolonged grief.

Mindfulness and exercise can help you feel better by deliberately manipulating how your body feels, but you also need to focus on the fuel your body uses for all of your activities, including meditation and exercise. It would be unrealistic to suggest that you can feel better with mindfulness practice and exercise if your eating habits don't reflect your commitment to self-care. Practicing regular meditation and exercise but eating doughnuts and ice cream all day is hardly wellness! Fortunately, building on your work in previous chapters, you can use the increased somatosensory awareness you've gained through mindfulness meditation and a health-promoting exercise regimen to establish and maintain good eating habits. This is a crucial piece in what I see as the four pillars of well-being: mindfulness practice, healthy sleep, regular exercise, and a healthful diet.

Eating Well

For many people in our culture, the word "diet" means a quick weight-loss plan. There are hundreds to choose from, ranging from low-carbohydrate, high-protein diets to entirely plant-based vegan diets. In this book, I use the term "diet" to mean the food you're choosing to eat, rather than a weight-loss plan or other nutritional fad.

Your diet is composed of two equally important features: what you eat, and how much you eat. Both the quality and the quantity of the food you eat have a big influence how your body feels and how you feel about your body. With difficult mood states, such as depression and anxiety, people often have a poor *satiety signal*, meaning it's harder to tell when they're hungry or full.

Plus, when grief is intense, you may feel as though what you're eating isn't very important, as long as it does the job of meeting your basic needs. With prolonged grief, few people are able to maintain either a healthy weight or healthy eating habits. You may have lost a lot of weight in your grief or, at the other extreme, you may have gained quite a bit. Not knowing when you're hungry or full and eating out of convenience or necessity rather than for health can take a profound toll on your body and mind over time.

The satiety signal becomes impaired because the body is releasing a steady stream of the stress hormone cortisol. Normally, cortisol is produced in short bursts throughout the day, with the highest level in the morning, just upon awakening, and the lowest level after you go to sleep at night. This helps give you energy to start the day and prepare your body for breakfast after sleeping. When faced with chronic stress, including prolonged grief, your body steadily releases higher levels of cortisol. Over time, this can weaken your immune system, alter your sleep cycle, and increase your blood pressure. It can also make you crave sweets. Part of what cortisol does is alter how the body maintains blood sugar levels in order to give you quick energy. When cortisol levels are chronically high, the body may crave carbohydrates or sweets, as they are most easily converted into blood sugar. It's not a coincidence that what we normally think of as comfort foods tend to be high in carbohydrates and laden with sugar.

Fortunately, regular exercise can help regulate the pattern of cortisol release. You can help the process along—and help your mood—by making more conscious food choices. Diet can have a profound impact on mood, and, conversely, mood can have a profound impact on diet.

A recent study (Davison and Kaplan 2012) found that people experiencing mood disorders, such as depression, tend to eat fewer healthful foods, such as whole grains, vegetables, and fruits, than others. This means you may find yourself eating more foods that are high in fat, sugar, and salt or more processed meat—again, comfort foods. You may not be surprised to learn that in the sample of people studied, almost half of those who were depressed tended to eat meals not prepared at home. Of course, restaurant meals and fast food are typically higher in fat, sugar, and salt. As a consequence, most of the people in this study who were depressed also had higher cholesterol levels.

As you can see from this study, the combination of depression and poor diet can have devastating consequences on long-term health. My hope is that by practicing mindfulness meditation regularly and exercising frequently, you'll develop a greater level of awareness of your body and its needs, and that this will help you make healthier choices about the food you eat.

To promote healing at all levels, you need to make sure you're putting healthful fuel into your body, choosing meals based on the greater somatosensory awareness you've developed as a result of meditation and exercise. Your mindful awareness will also aid you in noticing the difference in how your body feels as a result of the food choices you make.

The practices in this chapter will help you devote more mindfulness to the health choices you make at every meal. I recommend that you read through them first, and then begin to practice them as often as you wish.

✦ ✦ ✦ practice:
Eating with Gratitude

In many Buddhist traditions, people extend gratitude for all of the hard work that went into each meal before eating. This practice can also help you be more mindful of your meals and the food choices that you're making. It will help you consider the sources of your food and how it has been processed. In general, the more healthful the ingredients and processing methods (if any), the more healthful the meal will be for you.

As with any mindfulness exercise, make sure your television and phone are off before you begin. Although you may have been trying your best to avoid silence during meals because it heightens your loneliness, this practice involves eating with presence and thankfulness rather than fear, stress, or distraction. If difficult emotions come to the surface, observe them as they try to dominate your experience, and watch how they fade away as you bring your awareness back to belly breathing and being present for the meal you are eating.

In Buddhist traditions, it's also common to dedicate enjoyment of the meal to all beings that they may share and benefit from it. This allows you to fully experience the delicious flavors and health-giving properties of the food in a way that perpetuates the interconnected processes that brought the food to your table. You become the recipient of a complex supply chain and also the hub in extending your potential outward for the benefit of others. You are no longer eating in isolation, but as a participant in an infinitely complex web of being. Even a simple meal is part of everything that goes into it and comes out of it.

Before you begin to eat, take three mindful belly breaths as you gaze at the food before you. Place your hands a few inches over the food and thank all of the hard work that went into getting this food to you. You can thank the farmers, the farmhands, the truck drivers, the grocers, and whoever purchased the food and prepared the meal. If you're eating meat, you can also thank the animal for giving up its life to sustain yours.

If you say a prayer before meals in your faith tradition, you can add something along the following lines after your prayer, to better focus your mindful awareness on the food you are about to eat: "I give thanks to all beings who allowed this meal to be put together to nourish my body, spirit, and mind. To all living things everywhere, I offer the enjoyment of this meal. May it provide me with the energy to practice wisdom and compassion for the benefit of all and myself."

✦ ✦ ✦

✦ ✦ ✦ practice:
Eating Mindfully

The legendary mindfulness meditation pioneer Jon Kabat-Zinn (1990) has used a mindful eating exercise as part of his instruction for decades. In his groups, participants are presented with a single raisin to eat mindfully. You can do this exercise by yourself, at home using the guidelines below. Be sure to wash your hands first, since you'll be eating with your fingers.

If you don't have any raisins, any single, bite-size morsel, such as a small piece of dried fruit or a nut, dried cherry, or cranberry works well. If you only have larger dried fruit, like dates, apricots, or figs, cut off a piece about the size of a raisin for this exercise. Place this near you for the meditation session. Read through all of the instructions for this exercise before you begin so you don't have to disturb your practice to refer to the book.

1. Get comfortable in your sitting meditation posture. Become aware of your surroundings, as you've become accustomed to doing in your meditation practice. Then bring your awareness to your body and breath.

2. Take twenty-one mindful breaths, silently counting the breath each time you exhale. If you keep losing count, do your best and aim to meditate on your breath for about ten minutes.

3. Place the dried fruit or whatever food you've chosen in your palm. Look at it mindfully. Notice its texture and its weight. Breathe for another twenty-one breaths while just looking at this tiny, single bite of food. As your mind wanders, return your gaze to the food in the palm of your hand.

4. Place the food in your mouth, between your front teeth. Don't start chewing right away. You can touch the back of the fruit gently with your tongue. Notice any

thoughts or feelings that arise. Does it feel strange to just have this piece of food between your teeth for so long? Take twenty-one breaths with this single bite between your front teeth, being mindful of its presence. Swallow any saliva you accumulate.

5. Start chewing slowly while maintaining your belly breathing. Count each time you chew, and try to chew at least ten times before you swallow. Notice the act of swallowing a single bite mindfully.

6. To complete this exercise, take another twenty-one mindful breaths. Be particularly aware of how your body feels after being nourished by a single bite.

It is surprising how immense a single bite can feel when eaten mindfully. Yet we so often shovel food into our mouths, bite after bite, without paying any attention to the food or the act of eating. If you've grown accustomed to eating unhealthy foods, this may be part of the reason.

After doing this practice, you can extend this approach to the first bite of any meal. In addition, you can begin your meal with the practice of eating with gratitude to heighten your awareness of the food you've chosen and dedicate the benefit of your experience of the meal for the enjoyment and benefit of all beings everywhere.

You may not always be able to take a full twenty-one breaths at each stage of your first bite of a meal, especially if you're eating in a public place. In such cases, you can take three mindful breaths instead. The important thing is to take the first bite of your meal mindfully. Make sure it's not too hot, then hold a bite inside your mouth for a moment without chewing it. Be mindful of each time you chew. Notice how the textures and flavors change each time. Notice how it feels to swallow the food. And notice how your body feels as it integrates the food into itself. Does your meal help you feel healthy? Does it feel good to digest this meal? How does your body feel after eating this meal?

Amidst the pain of prolonged grief, eating may have become just another mindless and undesired chore eclipsed by the pain of loneliness. You may have found yourself choosing convenience over sustenance. A lot of people going through grief find themselves dreading mealtimes, which often seem to highlight the sense of isolation that comes from losing a loved one. Mindful eating can help by turning your awareness to your meals, rather than the absence of your loved one. You'll be more focused on what is present during the meal rather than on what is absent. Instead of choosing to being distracted by the television during meals, you can begin to relearn how to enjoy your food.

✦ ✦ ✦

Healthy Food Choices

I'm sure that, like me, you have witnessed the rise and fall of countless health fads over the years. Low-carb, high-protein diets, vegan raw food diets, cabbage soup diets, and many others, even cookie diets, have claimed to be the secret to weight loss. Many of them have dubious nutritional value, so although you may lose weight, you probably won't be getting the balanced nutrition your body needs for long-term optimal health.

Of all the diets that have been hyped, one does have a lot of good scientific evidence behind it: the Mediterranean diet. Before I explain it, a word of caution: If you have particular dietary needs or concerns, stick to what works best for you. If that isn't a concern, let's take a look at what kind of foods would ideally be part of a more mindful approach to eating.

The Mediterranean diet has captured the attention of medical researchers since the 1940s. This type of diet was exemplified by people living on the island of Crete. At that time, because of local conditions left after World War II, the diet of Crete's denizens consisted of fresh wild greens, whole grains, fruits, vegetables, and legumes (peas, lentils, or beans). While the main source of fat was olive oil, most people ate a bit of cheese or yogurt every day. Very little red meat or poultry was available, so most people consumed these foods in only limited quantities, if at all. Their main source of animal protein was fish and other fresh seafood. They also drank red wine from time to time.

Notice what's missing in the Mediterranean diet. There is no fast food, no drive-through fare, no candy, and no ice cream or other rich desserts. There is no prepackaged or processed food or what Michael Pollan calls "foodlike substances" (2009, 1): things like sugary cereals, sweet yogurt drinks, nacho cheese sauce, microwave meals, or packaged snacks. Everything was made with natural, wholesome ingredients that your great-grandmother could have recognized.

Again, note that the Mediterranean diet that confers such impressive health benefits is composed of the types of foods and portion sizes that were typical in Crete, Greece, southern Italy, southern France, Spain, Portugal, and Morocco after the war (Keys 1995). Also note that, although we may idealize what the Mediterranean region is like, after World War II everyone there was touched by trauma and loss. Everyone knew someone who had died or been killed or displaced by the war. This was hardly the same landscape we see in tourism brochures today. In the many decades since World War II, the diets of people living in that region have changed, as has the region.

I personally try to follow a Mediterranean diet and limit my intake of animal-based proteins. I don't adhere to a low-carb diet, nor am I vegan, but my body seems to function better with whole grains, fruits, and especially leafy green vegetables like kale and collard greens. This type of lifestyle works well for me, and I feel more energetic and healthier when I eat this way. With this type of diet, each meal becomes a source of life-sustaining energy rather than something that seems to weigh me down. But again, if your physical health requires you to follow a different diet, please ignore the recommendation to try a Mediterranean diet.

Healthy Portions

In addition to being mindful of what you eat, you also should be aware of how much you eat. In the United States, we take pride in the abundance available to us. However, we usually consume portions in excess of what our bodies need. As a species, we have never had this combination of large portions of food, processed food, and a sedentary lifestyle available to us. The toll on our health has been staggering.

Many people don't know what healthy portion sizes are. If that applies to you, here are some guidelines. Please note that the following list shows the amount considered to be an adequate portion per meal:

◆ For meat, the size of a deck of cards

◆ For vegetables, the size of a baseball or your fist

◆ For grains, slightly smaller than a baseball

◆ For cheese, one and a half ounces, about the size of three dice

This gets complicated in that, although these recommendations may be true on average for each meal, you may consume more than a recommended portion of some foods at some meals and less at others. For instance, if you have a cheese sandwich on whole-grain bread, you may exceed the recommendation for how much cheese and bread you should have during a meal. However, if that's all the cheese and bread you eat that day, you're doing fine. In general, you can use the information I've given you to roughly estimate how much of each of the main food groups you should eat, but also remember to enjoy your food!

You can find more information about healthful portion sizes and recommended number of servings daily at the US Department of Agriculture's website www.choosemyplate.gov, under the "MyPlate" tab.

Putting It All Together

I generally like to make sure that my lunch or dinner is dominated by plant-based ingredients. The largest portion of each meal is usually a green salad with a little olive oil, or cooked greens and vegetables. Whole grains and beans, fish, cheese, or nuts typically make up the rest. Dessert is usually fruit and yogurt or cheese with honey. Breakfast is usually oatmeal or whole-grain bread with fruit or honey. Of course, these are only suggestions. Play around with a variety of healthful whole foods to see what you come up with for yourself. As time goes on, I believe you'll appreciate how much better your body feels more than you miss eating unhealthy foods.

Even if you have to eat different kinds of food than what I'm recommending here, you should know that regular exercise is also considered to be part of the Mediterranean diet. We usually don't think of activity as being part of a diet, but it is. While what you eat is important, what you do with the energy you put into your body in the form of food is also crucial. Eating a healthful diet will only get you so far if your lifestyle is sedentary. People living in the Mediterranean region after World War II didn't go to the gym, but they did get a lot of exercise. Most people couldn't afford cars, and even if they could, very little fuel was available. Therefore, most people had to walk or ride a bike to get anywhere. Like early monks, for these people physical activity was a necessity, not something they had to schedule.

I believe that another key component of the Mediterranean diet is taking joy in preparing and eating meals. Since this diet doesn't include processed food, all meals are made from scratch and created with a spirit of celebration and pride in locally grown ingredients and the crafting of the meal, no matter how simple or complex. In the Mediterranean region in the years immediately after the war, the ingredients for each meal were local and seasonal foods, often grown or harvested by the family or friends or neighbors. This created enthusiasm about the quality and care that went into tending the land, catching the fish, pressing the olive oil, and so on.

In the following practice, which involves preparing a meal mindfully, you can experiment with the Mediterranean diet using ingredients that are usually easy to find. However, you can certainly extend this mindful approach to the preparation of any meal—hopefully one that's healthful!

✦ ✦ ✦ practice:
Preparing a Meal Mindfully

Perhaps you've never cooked by yourself, or maybe you stopped cooking after your loved one died. In either case, and even if you do cook your meals, I encourage you to reclaim your kitchen by preparing wholesome meals mindfully. For the purposes of this practice, I've included a simple recipe that can help nourish your body and, when prepared mindfully, can also help you feel present, rather than stressed about cooking. Take as many mindful breaths as you need to while cooking; no one is grading this meal. Consider it a mental exercise for engaging in the process of nourishing your body. If you like, make it a social event by inviting someone over. Mindful cooking is the opposite of fast food; the process of preparing the meal is just as important as the act of eating and the quality of the food.

Here are the ingredients you'll need:

- ✦ *1½ teaspoons salt*

- ✦ *6 to 8 ounces whole-grain spaghetti or other whole-grain pasta*

- ✦ *1 bunch fresh collard greens, kale, spinach, chard, or dandelion greens*

- ✦ *2 teaspoons olive oil*

- ✦ *1½ teaspoons finely chopped garlic*

- ✦ *3 tablespoons chopped fresh basil leaves, or 1 teaspoon dried basil*

- ✦ *1 (15-ounce) can chickpeas, lentils, or white beans, or 2 cups of cooked beans, rinsed and drained*

Before you start, take twenty-one mindful belly breaths in your kitchen. Be mindful that you will be nourishing your body with the wholesome food you're about to prepare.

Bring 2 quarts of water to a boil in a large pot over high heat. Add 1 teaspoon of the salt. Add the spaghetti and return to a boil. Lower the heat and cook, stirring occasionally, until the spaghetti is tender but still firm to the bite, usually 8 to 9 minutes. Drain well in a colander. Rinse under cold water for 10 seconds, then drain again.

Meanwhile, wash the greens, then rinse them thoroughly. Notice the sensation of the water meeting the greens as you wash them. Trim away the tough stems. Be mindful as you cut the leaves into 1-inch strips. Try exhaling each time you cut.

Clean and dry the pasta pot. Place it over medium-high heat. Once the pot is hot and completely dry, add the olive oil, and swirl the pot until the oil evenly coats the bottom. Add the garlic and stir once. Notice the sounds of cooking happening, such as the sound of garlic sizzling. Add the greens and the remaining ½ teaspoon of salt. While inhaling, stir once. As you exhale, stir again. Cook, stirring constantly, until the greens start to wilt.

Stir in the basil. Notice how the smell of the meal changes. Add the chickpeas and stir until well mixed and heated through. Add the pasta and mix gently just until the greens are incorporated into the spaghetti.

Transfer to a large serving bowl or plates. You may have enough for a few servings; the leftovers can be your convenience food. Now you can sit down to eat.

With this prepared meal in front of you, notice your posture. Make any corrections necessary to maintain good posture. As you look at the completed meal, take three belly breaths.

Before eating, observe the practice of eating with gratitude, thanking all who participated in bringing the meal to you and extending the benefits of the meal outward. Take your first bite mindfully, as in the mindful eating practice.

✦ ✦ ✦

✦ ✦ ✦ practice:
Cleaning Up Mindfully

A necessary part of every meal is cleaning up afterward. If you haven't been preparing meals regularly, cleaning up afterward may feel quite strange. Perhaps your loved one usually did the cleanup, or perhaps you did it together. There is also the awkward pain of cleaning up after one less person. Perhaps the act of washing dishes in some way emphasizes the absence of your loved one, just as cooking for one fewer person does.

Approaching cleaning up mindfully can help neutralize some of this distress. You can do this practice as a continuation of the other mindful eating practices in this chapter, putting them all together for an extended experience of mindfulness before, during, and after your meal.

Cleaning up after a meal can become a mindful exercise simply by bringing awareness to your breath and posture while you clear the table, wash dishes, and deal with garbage. Begin by taking three mindful breaths after you finish your meal. Then walk your dishes over to the sink. Take a deep belly breath as you reach for the faucet. As you exhale, turn the faucet on. Notice the water and your breath both being released. Try to maintain belly breathing as you wash all of the dishes.

You might also repeat mindful phrases to yourself, for example, "As I clean these dishes which held my meal, may my mind also become cleansed and renewed" or "May the nourishment of this meal allow me to practice wisdom and compassion toward myself and others."

If you turn your awareness to belly breathing and the physical process of cleaning up, this often automatic task can become part of a deliberate mindful meditation on sustenance, compassion, and health.

◆ ◆ ◆

Summary

In my personal and clinical experience, when people eat more mindfully in tandem with a sitting mindfulness practice and regular exercise, they become more attuned to how both healthful and unhealthful foods affect their body. Your mind and body will both feel different after you eat an apple than after you eat a doughnut or candy bar. Being more mindfully aware of how your food choices affect you is another important step toward well-being and taking care of yourself during prolonged grief—and beyond.

I hope the practices in this chapter, and throughout this book, can help you transition away from doing activities in the foggy autopilot of emotional pain and toward deliberate, conscious awareness and taking charge of your life. To that end, the next chapter explores how you can bring mindfulness to routine, day-to-day chores.

+ + +

CHAPTER 7

Mindful Cleaning and Decluttering

At this point, you've practiced mindfulness as a sitting meditation and also as a vehicle for facilitating more healthful sleep, regular exercise routines, and healthier eating habits. The goal behind this rigorous and comprehensive approach to mindfulness is to help you feel more empowered and to experience greater well-being, even if you still have times of intense emotional pain. Hopefully these painful times are becoming less frequent and intense, and also less exhausting.

The more you practice mindfulness meditation, the more your brain is likely to become sensitive to the needs of your body, which will help you establish a healthy lifestyle that prioritizes physical and emotional well-being. By engaging in the healthful practices you've been exploring, you're likely to experience a steady but significant improvement in how you're feeling. By nurturing your mind with meditation and your body with adequate sleep, movement, and nutrition, you may begin to experience a more unified mind-body relationship based on wellness and rejuvenation. This is going to start feeling a world apart from the sluggishness and heaviness of grief.

Doing Chores Mindfully

Mindfulness can also be practiced during everyday chores, transforming mundane and sometimes tedious tasks into opportunities to experience well-being, peace, and compassion for your weary mind. Take, for example, the practice of cleaning up mindfully in the previous chapter. Once you have a steady sitting practice and are engaged in other wellness-based activities, you can begin to transform tasks you've been doing automatically for a long time into additional vehicles for mindfulness practice.

Monastic Traditions

For many thousands of years, mindfulness was practiced primarily by monks and nuns in Buddhist societies. They lived in monasteries of all sizes—some the size of large universities, and others single small buildings no bigger than a typical American home. Many years ago, I visited Lhasa, the capital of Tibet. A few miles outside of the city is the large Drepung Monastery. In its heyday, before the Chinese invaded in the 1950s, this large monastic university housed up to ten thousand monks. Walking through the alleyways and large kitchens of the monastery was like walking through the streets of a medieval town. The monk who was showing me around said that in the old days, all of the necessary functions of the monastery were carried out by fellow monks. From cooks to repairmen and even to police, all were monks engaged in Buddhist study and practice in some capacity, many of them raised at the monastery since childhood.

Every morning before dawn, monks charged with preparing breakfast would rise to light fires under giant kettles for Tibetan salted butter tea and large pans for roasting barley flour, called *tsampa*, for hot cereal to warm up in the chill of mornings at the twelve-thousand-foot altitude of the monastery. Other monks were charged with cleaning the pots and pans and the dishes of the others—up to ten thousand monks! To guard against conflict or monks oversleeping, police monks armed with large whips performed rounds, keeping order and making sure the rules of the monastery were being followed.

Of course, not all monks were meditation masters. However, I like to think that for some of the monks assigned to the necessary chores of the monastery, everyday tasks became part of their meditation practice. In every monastic tradition, tasks required to keep large gatherings of people neat and orderly were colored with the practice of meditation and prayer. This was also evident in the Christian monastic traditions of Europe and North Africa, where the earliest church fathers practiced in austerity amid bleak surroundings, their monastic communities maintained by fellow monks and seekers.

Training with Ordinary Chores

The Tibetan Buddhist tradition that I'm familiar with is filled with stories of sages who go to great lengths to meet famous spiritual masters only to be told to do menial labor before learning anything else. The story of the famous Tibetan saint Milarepa, whose teacher, Marpa Lotsawa, required him to build, knock down, and rebuild a tower several times, stands out. By now, you may not be surprised to learn that at the heart of Milarepa's life was a deep sorrow and profound grief from losing his father at an early age and the circumstances that followed.

Milarepa was born into a wealthy family. When he was a child, his father died and his aunt and uncle stole all of his father's estate, leaving young Milarepa and his mother destitute. At the urging of his mother, Milarepa learned sorcery to avenge their losses. He used his power to cause giant hailstorms that collapsed a house on top of his aunt and uncle during a celebration and ruined the crops of everyone in the village who had mistreated his mother and himself. Dozens were killed outright, and many more were displaced by the famine that followed.

Filled with remorse, Milarepa eventually went to find Marpa, the legendary translator of Buddhist texts from Sanskrit into Tibetan. Before Marpa would teach him anything, he commanded Milarepa to build a large tower. Milarepa obliged. Finding this tower unsatisfactory, Marpa then asked him to tear it down and build a new one. Milarepa obliged. Then Marpa did the same thing again. Marpa approved the third and final version, but to Milarepa it seemed as though there was still no spiritual teaching bestowed upon him.

Frustrated by his lack of progress, Milarepa asked Marpa's wife for help. She forged a letter of introduction to another teacher for him, but Milarepa soon returned to Marpa, realizing that anything he learned under deceptive circumstances would be fruitless. Eventually, Marpa relented and taught Milarepa meditation techniques and wisdom that eventually led to his enlightenment.

Of course, this story is a bit melodramatic, and takes place a thousand years ago in the mountains and plains of Tibet. Still, there is wisdom in it. Before Milarepa could experience spiritual growth, he had to first engage in menial tasks such as construction, painting, and cleanup. The transformative potential of meditation practice wasn't presented to him on a silver platter. In fact, it began under the guise of hard physical labor. He literally had to build his practice with brick and mortar. It is humbling to think of one of the most famous and revered Tibetan saints doing anything but sitting in the cave retreat of his later years, singing the songs and poems he's famous for. Yet there he was, baking bricks, mixing mortar, hauling stones, sawing planks, and laying tile.

The point of this story is to illuminate how we often have preconceived notions of what spiritual growth looks like. Perhaps, like a lot of people, you think that mindfulness is only supposed to take place on a meditation cushion, maybe in some peaceful retreat in an exotic location. You may assume that peace of mind and spiritual growth exist at another place far removed from the realities of the pain of your everyday life. Many people I've met over the years make this mistake, thinking their meditation practice is separate from their everyday life, particularly mundane, day-to-day tasks.

Milarepa's story teaches us that menial tasks are not only an essential part of our lives, but also form the foundation of our spiritual growth. Sometimes ordinary tasks teach us extraordinary things—if we are mindful enough to pay attention. The renowned Chinese Zen master Xu Yun spoke of spending countless hours meditating only to have an enlightenment experience when some hot tea accidentally spilled on his hand during a meal. Of course, all of that meditating may have primed him to have an enlightenment experience, but it was the normal activities of everyday life—like drinking tea—that provided the opportunity for his bliss.

What the stories of Milarepa and Master Xu Yun teach is that meditation is part of the chores and tasks you do every day, not separate from them. It's tempting to fall into dualistic thinking about what is meditative and what isn't. People often think that mindfulness is a practice to engage in only during meditation, and then they can get up and do whatever else they need to do however they want. However, Milarepa and Master Xu Yun show how mindfulness can be mixed into all of our activities, not just sitting practice. Your pain has found a way to creep into the ordinary tasks of your life. Why not allow mindfulness to do the same?

Hopefully the exercises in the previous chapter helped you develop moments of cooking mindfully, eating mindfully, and cleaning up mindfully. If so, you've already learned that tasks you usually do automatically can be very centering.

In the same way, sweeping, vacuuming, cleaning, and organizing can also be transformed into mindfulness exercises that contribute to your well-being. With mindful awareness, virtually any action can provide a meaningful opportunity for wellness. This approach to accomplishing tasks is practiced at many meditation retreat centers. However, you don't have to travel a great distance or spend a lot of money for an extended retreat to do everyday chores mindfully. You can start in your own home, right where you are.

✦ ✦ ✦ practice:
Sweeping Mindfully

A common household chore is sweeping the floor. At your home, this may be indoors or outside on a deck, balcony, or steps. Sweeping mindfully has a long history in the Buddhist tradition, probably since it needs to be done often in the dusty environments in which so many Buddhist monasteries are located.

1. To sweep mindfully, begin by standing with your broom.

2. Check your posture: Is your back erect but not too tight? Are you holding the broom handle comfortably and at an angle that won't cause pain later?

3. Now take some belly breaths. I like to start chores with three mindful breaths, pausing briefly after each inhalation and exhalation.

4. Look down at the ground you're about to sweep. Think of the ground as a living being that will be overjoyed at being cleaned up, like a puppy after a bath.

5. Position the broom on the floor away from your body and hold it steady. As you inhale, bring the broom toward your body, sweeping up dirt along the way.

6. As you exhale, lift the broom and move it away from your body, finding the next spot to clean.

7. As you inhale, put the broom on the floor and draw it back close to you, observing the cleaner surface it leaves behind.

8. Repeat this process until you've swept up what you need to, inhaling as you bring the broom close to your body, and exhaling as you move the broom away again.

9. Do this task mindfully, timing the movement of the broom with each relaxed, unforced breath.

In a short time, you may find that you're deeply relaxed. Again, think of the ground as a living being, overjoyed at and grateful for being cleaned. You may also think of each of your breaths as sweeping away any distressing or negative emotions from your mind and body, gathering all of your sorrow into a pile and leaving the ground clean. Your breath and the broom have something in common in this mindful task: both are purifying and cleansing the areas they touch.

Sweeping is one of my favorite tasks to do mindfully. Of course, it can take much longer than sweeping on autopilot. But notice how different it feels. Who knew sweeping could become such a profoundly moving ritual? You can also use this technique for mopping or raking leaves.

◆ ◆ ◆

◆ ◆ ◆ practice:
Vacuuming and Decluttering Mindfully

Vacuuming, like sweeping, is probably also something you have to do regularly. You can apply a similar approach to this routine chore:

1. To vacuum mindfully, bring your vacuum cleaner to the area you need to clean. Plug it into the wall, but don't turn it on just yet.

2. Stand behind the vacuum and take three mindful belly breaths, slowly and rhythmically. Notice your posture. Make sure your posture is erect and your back isn't tight. You may need to relax your knees so you aren't hunched over.

3. Notice the dirt and debris on the rug or carpet in front of you. If you notice that there's a lot of dust and dirt on the rug, become mindful of how dusty your mind can feel at times, as well.

4. Turn on the vacuum cleaner.

5. As you exhale, push the vacuum cleaner away from you. Notice the pattern of clean carpet it leaves behind. As you inhale, move the vacuum cleaner back toward you and again notice the clean carpet left behind.

6. Repeat, exhaling as the vacuum cleaner moves away from you to clean the area next to the one you just did. Notice the pattern it makes, overlapping with what you have already cleaned.

7. Repeat until you've vacuumed the entire area.

8. Once you've finished the job, turn off the vacuum cleaner. Stand behind the vacuum and observe the room. Notice how much cleaner it is.

9. If you notice that there's a lot of clutter in the area, become mindful of this. Is everything you have necessary? If not, pick up one thing that you know you don't need or don't want and either discard it or set it aside to donate, as appropriate.

10. You can do this every time you vacuum. Sometimes you may find that once you start looking at the clutter, you choose more things to sort through and donate or throw away.

After doing this practice, notice how you feel. How does it feel to have less clutter and fewer unnecessary things around?

✦ ✦ ✦

Your Loved One's Belongings

You can skip this section if you don't have any of your loved one's belongings or if you have only those belongings that you wish to keep.

For many people suffering from prolonged grief, one of the most difficult choices is what to do with a loved one's belongings. Sometimes this dilemma is settled by forces beyond your control, such as someone else being in charge of your loved one's possessions or having to immediately relocate after your loved one's death.

If you lived with your loved one or have a lot of his or her things, I'd like you to be mindful of practicing belly breathing while you read this section. Contemplating your loved one's belongings and what to do with them can trigger a lot of stress for a variety of reasons. No matter what the cause, stress usually feels the same. But it isn't mandatory.

Practice at least a few belly breaths before you continue reading.

Like many people, you may have found that after the bureaucracy following your loved one's death, you were simply too exhausted to sort out your loved one's belongings. As time went by, the weight of grief may have grown heavier, robbing you of any emotional and physical energy you may have had to sort out stuff. Before you knew it, months or maybe even years passed. At this point, you may have gotten used to having all of your loved one's stuff around. This stuff may have become not only symbolic of who your loved one was, but also of your prolonged grief.

People have different ideas about whether keeping many of a loved one's belongings is healthy. Many people feel that there's a certain period of time, be it weeks or months, in which it's legitimate to hold on to items that may be insignificant. I don't hurry my patients to get rid of things unless they feel it's necessary or those belongings are interfering with their lives and other relationships. Of course, it's a different issue if you have to move or if the sheer quantity of your loved one's belongings is crowding your living space.

For many people, a loved one's belongings were a part of their everyday surroundings and remain that way after the loved one dies. Perhaps you lost a spouse or a child, and his or her room, clothes, and bed remain in your home. The most personal items, like the pillow your loved one last used or dirty clothes that still carry his or her scent can trigger some of the most vivid memories and sharpest pain in your journey with grief.

Each object tells a story of how it was used and the person who used it, and each story churns up different feelings. It may feel pleasant to revisit these memories and stay connected to your loved one through these possessions. You may feel as though it is still your loved one's home as long as his or her things are there. A widow I worked with years ago once told me she didn't want to move or get rid of any of her husband's belongings because she felt as though he could still find his way to her as long as his stuff was there. She thought he might not be able to recognize the house without all his stuff inside it.

This may not sound logical. After all, wouldn't his spirit or soul want to be closer to her spirit, rather than to his old muscle cars and tools? But the emotional reality of her theory is inescapable. You may have your own theories about your loved one's belongings or afterlife. Or you may simply want to preserve your loved one's life by preserving his or her things. You may even be telling yourself your loved one is about to come home any day now, even though deep down you know this won't be happening. Material objects sometimes become symbolic connections to memories and relationships, extensions of a body that is no longer with us. This is completely natural and isn't inherently problematic. Sometimes, though, it can become a problem.

✦ ✦ ✦ practice:
Exploring Your Relationship to Your Loved One's Belongings

Like reading the preceding section, doing this practice may be a bit stressful. Please practice belly breathing as you answer the following questions:

What compels you to hold on to your loved one's belongings?

_____

_____

_____

What do you fear would happen if you got rid of your loved one's things?

_____

_____

_____

Do you feel like you should have less of your loved one's things around?

_____

Which single one of your loved one's possessions is most important to you?

✦ ✦ ✦

✦ ✦ ✦ practice:
Exploring Whether Keeping Your Loved One's Things Is Problematic

In psychology, we often look at different thoughts and behaviors in terms of their potential outcomes. One of the most consistent criteria in trying to distinguish behavior that's problematic from behavior that's appropriate is to ask whether what you're doing gets in the way of your life. Here are some questions to consider when deciding whether you should get rid of some of your loved one's things:

- *Are your loved one's belongings getting in the way of your ability to move around the house?*

- *Are your loved one's belongings getting in the way of your ability to do normal things, like working, cleaning, cooking, grooming, or bathing?*

- *Do people you respect comment on how much of your loved one's things you seem to have, excluding pictures?*

- *Do you feel like you should have gotten rid of more stuff by now?*

- *Are you embarrassed to have people over because of the number of things you have that belonged to your loved one?*

- *Does having your loved one's belongings around keep you from accomplishing your goals?*

If you answered yes to at least three of these questions, you should probably find a way to reduce the amount of stuff you have in general, including your loved one's belongings.

How Long to Hold On

A question that often comes up when I'm speaking with someone who's grieving is how long it's appropriate to hold on to a loved one's belongings. I don't think there's a standard time frame that applies to everyone. Even as a mental health care professional, I often don't feel like I can offer specific guidance here. How can I tell a family who lost a child that they should dismantle the child's bedroom? If it doesn't bother anyone or get in the way of everyday life, why is it a problem?

I think it's much more helpful to think of whether holding on to your loved one's things is healthy, rather than thinking about how long you've kept these things. Asking yourself what you think would be a healthy amount of time to hold on to your loved one's things is just part of the equation. Every situation is unique, every relationship different, and the loss of a particular person presents its own challenges. Go by what works for you, not by what someone else thinks is right.

I do recommend, however, that you explore this question after sitting in mindfulness meditation for fifteen minutes. Whenever the issue of your loved one's belongings comes up, you may get pretty stressed and therefore react—and sometimes overreact—automatically, without thinking through what your goals are for yourself. Grief takes over with its own priorities here, just as it does in other aspects of your life.

✦ ✦ ✦ practice:
Mindfully Considering Your Loved One's Possessions

Pause here to practice a few belly breaths and then engage in mindfulness meditation for fifteen minutes. Then come back to the book and continue reading.

✦ ✦ ✦

Now that you've calmed and centered yourself with a little formal mindfulness meditation, ask yourself these questions:

♦ *Do I need to keep everything I'm holding on to?*

- *Now that I'm more relaxed, can I think of any belongings that I might get rid of?*

- *How much time do I think is reasonable to hold on to my loved one's things?*

- *Does holding on to all this stuff help me heal?*

◆　◆　◆

What to Do with Your Loved One's Things

Eventually, some people find that only a few things—a necktie or T-shirt, a book or Bible, a souvenir or a favorite piece of jewelry—are enough. Many people decide to pack one small, carry-on size suitcase of possessions and either sell, donate, or throw away the rest. It might seem quite strange, even absurd: your entire experience of another human being, someone who means so much to you, packaged in a small suitcase. But remember, the memories don't belong to your loved one's things. Memories are what you carry within you, always.

It doesn't have to be all or nothing. You can keep a few tokens and get rid of the rest.

It might seem like it will feel bizarre—too strange—to be in your home without your loved one's belongings. Most people tell me that it doesn't feel as bad or as weird as they feared. Sometimes it actually feels liberating. Many people find it beneficial to have fewer physical triggers for grief's painful emotions.

Again, though, if your loved one's belongings aren't taking up too much space, don't get in the way of your everyday life, and don't trigger the sharp pain of grief, maybe they aren't a problem.

Practical Considerations

If you have a lot of things you want to get rid of, including big things like cars or a piano, I suggest you research services in your area that will haul them away and either donate or sell them. Some of these services will haul away whatever you ask them to. Various charities are often willing to come by and pick up items such as clothing or even furniture. Also consider contacting local churches or other places of worship to see if they take items to distribute to those in need.

Personally, I feel that one of the best uses for a loved one's possessions is to allow them to ease the lives of people who are struggling to meet their basic needs for survival. Donating your loved one's belongings to such people can be tremendously beneficial and serve as a profound memorial to your loved one. Wouldn't it feel good to know that your loved one is continuing to touch people's lives by helping people in need? Compassion and charity are often the best and most virtuous ways to deal with a loved one's belongings.

My experience has been that most charities, especially those that will haul away belongings for you, have specific guidelines on what they can accept. If you wind up with a lot of stuff you can't get rid of, you may want to have a yard sale.

If you decide to have a yard sale, be committed to it. You'll probably have second thoughts about getting rid of some items, or you may feel that you aren't charging enough based on your emotional attachment to your loved one's possessions. Committing to a yard sale means you'll have to respect your own decision to get rid of things that are getting in the way of how you envision the rest of your life. Try to think of it this way: it's not that you're losing things; it's that you're gaining more space, both literally and metaphorically.

If, after reading and working through this section, you feel more comfortable about distributing or discarding your loved ones belongings, don't hesitate. Take a deep belly breath, put the book down, and start working on solutions to decluttering your home.

Summary

Grief often challenges you to think outside of categories like right versus wrong. Instead, you may have to choose the most desirable out of what feel like only bad options. Over the years, I've found that most people experiencing prolonged grief struggle with the issue of what to do with their loved one's belongings. Sorting through your loved ones' things is a vivid reminder of this new equation you have to negotiate in life and with your grief. Remember, it's not a question of what you're *supposed* to be doing in your journey with grief. Rather, you're finding a path forward that can help you free yourself from the confines of grief and help you live your life with as much wellness as you can.

Up to this point in the book, you've learned a lot of techniques that can help you manage the stress of grief and wrestle with some very difficult choices. In the next chapter, you'll learn techniques to help you soothe some of the emotional pain of your loss. Just as dealing with your loved one's belongings addresses physical aspects of your loss, learning to soothe yourself compassionately can help you deal with some of the emotional aspects of your suffering.

CHAPTER 8

✦ ✦ ✦

Transforming Pain

In your work with this book, you've learned a lot of different skills and techniques built upon the practice of mindfulness meditation. You may have found mindfulness to be a centering, relaxing addition to your lifestyle. Hopefully you've also been able to alter your immediate surroundings and your eating, sleeping, and exercise patterns to create a life that's more conducive to your overall health and well-being. Practicing all of these techniques can help you feel a lot better, or at least not feel as miserable. You may notice that your ability to savor and enjoy pleasurable moments is growing, or at least notice more moments when you aren't in as much pain.

Mindfulness and Compassion

Let's now turn toward the common theme underlying all of the practices you've learned up to this point and all of the changes that you're working to implement in your life. Soothing your pain and alleviating your suffering are about compassion. Sitting with your mind and being present with the relaxing practice of belly breathing as you let any and every thought, feeling, and sensation rise and fall teaches you how to be open with yourself. This openness eventually begins to feel very welcoming. In the practice of mindfulness, you let go of judgment about what you're thinking, feeling, or noticing and are simply present with an attitude of acceptance.

Over time, you begin to identify more with your mindful self than all of your random thoughts—thoughts you may not even have realized you were having and that left you feeling more miserable. By welcoming everything without judgment, this mindful self feels centered and grounded. It feels a lot like a mind full of unconditional love—witnessing the experience of being yourself, and sharing that experience, without judgment, criticism, or distress. This awareness is like having the kind of parent we all wish we could have, or perhaps a parent we had when we needed them most, inside our minds.

Although each mindfulness meditation session may not have a specific goal aside from sitting practice, the practice of mindfulness is aimed at a specific intention. This intention is compassion. Sitting with unconditional acceptance as parts of the mind constantly race off in different directions and gently calling them back over and over again nurtures a part of the mind that soothes itself, like a patient parent works with a mischievous child. Mindfulness meditation teaches you to be patient with your mind, and this patience can ultimately lead to a transformative compassion for yourself and others.

Compassion starts with agreeing to sit down with yourself to try to figure out a way to heal through all of the hurt and suffering you're experiencing. Learning how to soothe yourself and find a place to put the pain so it doesn't burn you up or drive other people away is a compassionate intention. Mindfulness definitely can't change the events of your life and what has happened to you, but it can give you choices—compassionate choices—about how to live out the rest of the life you have.

The Awakening Mind

Mindfulness practitioners have long recognized and strived to harness the healing power of compassion. In the Buddhist tradition, there's a concept known as *bodhichitta*. It literally means "awakening mind"—the aspect of the mind that practices meditation and ultimately becomes completely enlightened. Bodhichitta is also often considered to be synonymous with compassionate mind.

These meanings are interrelated because, for a very long time, enlightenment and compassion have been observed to go hand in hand. Think of all of the most spiritually evolved people you can, such as Buddha, Jesus, Saint Francis, Mother Teresa, and the Dalai Lama. We revere them not only because we're taught to, but also because of the extraordinary compassion they display toward others, especially those who are frequently rejected.

But remember this: Their potential for enlightenment is no different from yours. These luminaries emphasize to us again and again that they are simply tapping into something we can all access. The compassion they show us is something we can all show to each other. They seem to be telling us that enlightenment is within reach, but only if compassion is present.

✦ ✦ ✦ practice:
Awakening Compassion

For this mindfulness practice, visualize the cutest creature you can think of, perhaps a puppy, kitten, baby koala, or baby panda. Visualize your mind as this cute creature. As you practice mindfulness during this exercise, count your breaths. Whenever you notice your thoughts getting out of hand or that you've lost count, imagine that this cute creature has run off, away from you. As you begin counting your breaths again, imagine that this creature has come back to rest in your lap. Try to keep it in your lap, focusing on counting each breath.

Notice how different it feels to envision your mind as a cute, helpless creature with good intentions, rather than as a frustrating chatterbox inside your head. Notice that your physical sensations change when you think of a cute animal. You probably find yourself more relaxed, and you may be smiling. Imagine you could have that feeling toward yourself when you think of yourself. This is what mindfulness attempts to lay the foundation for: self-love that isn't selfish or self-centered, but focused on giving and sharing itself.

✦ ✦ ✦

What Is Compassion?

Over the years, I've found that a lot of people have misconceptions about what compassion is. Therefore, I'd like to clarify this topic so that you and I are operating on the same understanding.

A common misconception is that compassion is the domain of special people—great people to idolize and revere, not ordinary folks like us. The Dalai Lama, Mother Teresa, Gandhi—those types of people can practice compassion. Other people get angry, lose their patience, or simply can't be around so much suffering.

This isn't true. Compassion isn't a quality that certain people have and others don't. Nearly everyone can generate compassion, and nearly everyone can benefit from being compassionate. To be clear, having compassion doesn't mean that you're incapable of feelings like anger, frustration, or depression from time to time. Even Jesus lost his patience at the merchants in Herod's temple.

Like many other rewarding aspects of life, compassion doesn't require pristine, perfect conditions. When you're experiencing intense emotional pain, you crave soothing. You may be longing for the presence of your deceased loved one, and your pain may be inflamed by knowing that your loved one isn't coming back and cannot soothe you. You may feel very alone in your pain, as if no one could possibly understand what you're going through and what you've already suffered in your journey with grief.

You are longing for compassion and love, not for pity. Compassion is not pity. Compassion is much more active. Compassion has a connotation of being something experienced together—something that someone gives to you or that you give to someone else. It means being motivated to help someone who is suffering, not just feeling sorry for that person or watching the person's suffering from afar.

Ultimately, mindfulness helps facilitate an expansion of compassion in our lives. This may sound a bit strange, since we think of compassion as being heart centered, whereas mindfulness sounds more like it's in the mind. Furthermore, we often assume that the mind and heart are opposites, frequently in conflict with each other. Yet we feel best when they are connected to each other.

Compassion relies on being able to share the open and welcoming awareness of your mindfulness practice with others. You may notice that as your practice of mindfulness deepens, you have an easier time extending this welcoming attitude toward both others and yourself. This is what compassion is all about: being able to move toward a better way of living through your pain, a way of living that can alleviate both your own pain and the pain and suffering of others.

Your grief is not yours alone; it affects everyone around you, no matter how close or distant you are from them. Your grief may have caused you to move away from certain relationships that mattered or toward new relationships that feel more comfortable. Or it may be depriving others of your company, perhaps friends you have yet to make or relationships that could have developed. Your grief doesn't happen in isolation, no matter how lonely you might feel. Therefore, your healing can also affect those around you in a positive way, no matter how close or distant you are from them.

To feel empowered to live more mindfully and compassionately, don't expect that you must work on major problems, like poverty or world hunger, in order to feel a sense of satisfaction or accomplishment. Compassion has many different contexts. It can start simply, with how we treat other people that we see regularly, perhaps in stores or restaurants. It can mean letting someone get ahead of you in traffic or helping someone who's lost. These small acts of kindness may feel a little strange, even silly, but eventually they will help you feel like a kind person who's connected to others and therefore matters in the world. This can alleviate the feeling that you're suffering alone.

✦ ✦ ✦ practice:
Engaging in Random Acts of Kindness

Connecting with other people compassionately several times a day just feels good. Each day, try to think of at least three ways you were kind and compassionate in a situation where you otherwise might not have been or didn't need to be. Write down with whom this happened, where, and what you did that was compassionate.

The person might be someone working in a store or restaurant, someone at work, a friend or family member, or someone in any other situation where you're around other people, such as on a bus or at church or temple. If you're seldom physically around other people, think of other ways of interacting, perhaps through social media such as Facebook or Twitter, by e-mail or phone, and so on. Alternatively, if you're not interacting with other people regularly, you might take this as a message that you need to get out of your home and spend more time doing things around others, if you're comfortable doing that.

If you can't think of three ways that you were kind to others, then think of three ways you could have been kinder or more compassionate. Change can't begin without insight, so with this approach at least you'll be taking a step toward insight. But remember, this is an exercise about compassion, not guilt. Use this approach to guide your future behavior, not ruminate about the past.

To help you get started, I've provided a tracking chart. Fill the chart out for three weeks so you can be sure that you've been acting on this intention for a while. The hope is that by tracking your compassionate actions for three weeks, they will become more second nature and you'll become more mindful of them. This will help perpetuate your compassion. By becoming more aware of your compassionate actions, over time you'll be more likely to see new situations in which you can apply a more compassionate approach.

Week 1	Sunday	Monday	Tuesday	Wednesday	Thursday	Friday	Saturday
Situation 1 Who Where What							
Situation 2 Who Where What							
Situation 3 Who Where What							

Week 2	Sunday	Monday	Tuesday	Wednesday	Thursday	Friday	Saturday
Situation 1 Who Where What							
Situation 2 Who Where What							
Situation 3 Who Where What							

Week 3	Sunday	Monday	Tuesday	Wednesday	Thursday	Friday	Saturday
Situation 1 Who Where What							
Situation 2 Who Where What							
Situation 3 Who Where What							

This exercise will help you get more familiar with practicing compassion on a daily basis. In addition, it will help you feel like you're dealing with the world in a more meaningful and positive way, increasing your motivation to practice mindfulness and compassion regularly. It really comes down to the Golden Rule, which can feel so soothing in the midst of emotional pain and turmoil: treat others as you want yourself to be treated.

Three Levels of Mindfulness

Compassion has long been entwined with the practice of mindfulness. In the Buddhist literature, there is an understanding that mindfulness has three levels. The first level is simply awareness of the traffic in the mind—all of the urges and ruminations that you notice when you practice mindfulness. You're surely more aware by now that meditation doesn't require an empty mind; this first level is all of the mental chatter that you become aware of when you practice mindfulness. It's the first step of mindfulness practice, and like the first steps on any long journey, it is often the part that takes the most energy.

The second level is connecting your mind, heart, and body with your behavior. This means having a better understanding of how your thoughts, feelings, and behaviors are all interrelated. Hopefully mindfulness practice is helping you become more aware of the consequences of how you spend your time. As a result, you may be beginning to live a bit differently. This second level takes some deliberate effort, but not as much as the first level. In becoming more mindful of yourself, your behaviors naturally change, becoming more wholesome and health promoting. Your pain may still be there, but it isn't dictating all of your choices or dominating all of your time with the same intensity.

The third level of mindfulness is an intuitive union of mind, heart, and body. This level is the hardest to achieve and may take a while. However, once you reach this level, you don't need to exert much energy to maintain it. I suspect this is what happens after a few months of dedicated, disciplined mindfulness practice. I also suspect that this is what accounts for all of the neurological changes in those who practice mindfulness, as shown in various brain scan studies. At this level, your actions are almost automatically health promoting and informed by your mindfulness practice even when you aren't deliberately trying to be mindful. At this level, mindfulness is not only something you practice, but something you are.

I must clarify that even at the third level of mindfulness, you shouldn't expect your mind to be silent. It will still chatter away, trying to find dark corners filled with intense pain, petty concerns to churn into tension, or daydreams and fantasies that carry you away from mindful awareness. What changes is your attitude toward your mind, toward your heart and body, and toward others.

Paths to Becoming More Compassionate

Mindfulness teaches that compassion sometimes happens when you don't expect it. I firmly believe that one of the hidden treasures of mindfulness is developing a greater capacity for unconditional love toward yourself. This is where all compassion comes from. After all, how can you be compassionate toward others without first extending compassion toward yourself? Self-love is a vital ingredient for being compassionate.

The second ingredient may sound surprising to you: it is your pain. This may seem counterintuitive. You may assume that compassion is the opposite of your pain, that it requires being free of pain. But this is impossible.

Emotional pain has a self-absorbing quality that limits your awareness of others. You may have little interest in what seem to be petty problems or mundane dilemmas that other people are experiencing. What could possibly measure up to the loss that has caused you so much pain? But as the Tibetan Buddhist teacher Chögyam Trungpa Rinpoche (1993) has described it, our own open wounds are where our capacity to feel, and to feel for the pain of others, comes from. Compassion relies on your ability to feel emotional pain—first your own and then that of others. Compassion isn't the opposite of pain, but it can transform you in the midst of your pain.

The prolonged pain of your grief may give you something useful to share with others—not the intensity of the pain, but that closeness that comes only from sharing tears together and, more specifically, that cherishing of relationships that arises after you lose someone who is important to you. Think of the warmth from others you may have experienced in some of your difficult moments and how much better it can feel to have arms around you as you cry, or even just to have the presence of someone else close by when you feel emotionally vulnerable. You can be that soothing presence for yourself and others. This is part of what your pain can teach you about compassion.

Compassion for Your Pain

The wound of your grief is where your pain connects with the pain of others. What I've found in the Tibetan Buddhist tradition is an understanding that sometimes pain hurts less when we are open to it. This doesn't mean wallowing in suffering; it means feeling these dark feelings in the bright light of mindful acceptance. Within the acknowledgment of the pain and all of the limitations that the pain brings, you can begin to feel motivated to practice great compassion, for your own suffering and for everyone else who is suffering like you.

To feel better, we sometimes have to move into the pain in order to be soothed. If you try to get away from pain, you're still likely to suffer, and even so, you can't escape. Trying to get away from the pain is more likely to make you feel tense, stressed, and exhausted. I encourage you to see what you can learn by accepting the reality of your pain compassionately. As a reminder, this isn't about wallowing in your suffering. It's about seeing what happens once you can contain the pain in a net of compassion.

Chögyam Trungpa Rinpoche once told a story about walking to a monastery with his attendants (Chödrön 1997). On the way there, they passed a ferocious Tibetan mastiff, chained to a stick and guarding the path. These large dogs, often dreadlocked and unkempt, are a common sight on the Tibetan plateau, striking terror in everyone with their fierce barking and downright monstrous appearance.

As Trungpa Rinpoche and his party passed the dog, it broke free from its chain. Everyone froze in terror. Trungpa Rinpoche, acting in a moment of intuitive spontaneity, instead ran toward the dog. Confused, the dog turned and fled away from the group, never to bother them again.

Years ago, I had a similar experience during one of my runs through suburban Florida. One of the dogs in the neighborhood had gotten loose and started chasing me. I did the same thing—I turned around and ran toward the dog. You know what? It worked. I've also found that this can work with painful emotions: approaching them, rather than fleeing, seems to deprive them of their power and often eases the stress and tension that seem to automatically accompany emotional pain.

Compassion therefore often requires courage. It isn't always easy or the path of least resistance. Compassion is often not even close to being an automatic response. Even though it might sound soft and welcoming, compassion is often the hardest thing to do. Think of what happens when someone irritates you. If you're in traffic and someone cuts you off or seems to be driving carelessly, your first reaction might not be one of understanding. Most people get angry, maybe even violent. In these situations, compassion doesn't seem like it's even in the realm of possibility. As much as we might like for compassion to arise in every moment it can, like mindfulness, it takes quite a bit of discipline, training, and effort.

"Closure" and Unfinished Business

I'm sure you've heard about the concept of closure, and there's a good chance that you've read or heard that achieving closure is necessary in your grief. This concept has always baffled me, and it may have confused you too. Exactly what does "closure" mean? Is the idea that, once a loved one dies, we're supposed to aim for living as if they were never with us? Does closure mean we're never supposed to feel the pain of the loss again, even when songs come on in the supermarket that remind us of being with someone we've lost? Does closure simply mean that we've had a chance to say good-bye, even if we weren't able to at the time of a loved one's death?

To be honest, in my experience closure comes up more often in the popular media than it does in therapy. We often hear stories about people who are looking for closure by bringing a killer to trial, or reports that finding a missing loved one's remains will help a family find closure. But from these examples, closure sounds more like the point when grief can truly begin, once the details of a loss are understood or a sense of justice has been attained.

I prefer to think of completing unfinished business rather than achieving closure. Conveying thoughts, feelings, or wishes for your loved one that you weren't able to extend before your loved one died can definitely help you heal. There tend to be a few recurring types of unfinished business that people have with deceased loved ones. Ira Byock, MD (2004), a pioneer in hospice care, has written extensively on what he believes is most important in helping with unfinished business. I use his work and insights to help my patients quite often.

According to Dr. Byock, these are some of the more common types of unfinished business:

- Needing to express forgiveness

- Needing to be forgiven

- Expressing gratitude

- Expressing love

- Saying good-bye

All of these can be dealt with under the umbrella of wishing yourself and your loved one to be well and free from suffering.

I encourage you to think about closure as the point at which you feel like you can connect with the memory of your loved one with a feeling of love, rather than with only pain or distress. There may still be pain, but being able to feel anything other than pain is a liberating step in grief for many people. This often begins once any unfinished business is addressed.

Think of closure as what happens when you can show compassion for yourself in your grief and tap into feelings other than pain in regard to your loved one. I've found that the practice of loving-kindness meditation is extremely helpful in allowing this to happen.

Loving-Kindness

In Buddhist meditation, there are two different terms for compassion—*metta* and *karuna*. Metta, or loving-kindness, is the wish for others to be well, and karuna is the wish for others to be free of suffering. For the purposes of helping you in your grief, let's assume that compassion is composed of both in equal parts: for others to be well and free from suffering, just as you wish the same for yourself. As you may have guessed, you have to start with yourself and with the reasons you're working through this book: to be well and free from suffering to the greatest extent possible.

✦ ✦ ✦ practice:
Metta, or Loving-Kindness, Meditation

Read through this entire exercise before you sit down to practice it. If you have a timer or alarm, you can set it to chime every five to ten minutes to alert you to switch to the next part of the meditation.

Sit down in a quiet place where you can practice undisturbed for twenty to forty minutes. Begin by taking a few mindful breaths. Close your eyes and visualize your body. Think of yourself, your mind, your body, and your heart. Think of the uniqueness that goes into being you, the sense of being you.

As you imagine yourself, inhale and silently say these words to yourself:

May I be free from suffering.

As you exhale, silently say these words to yourself:

May I be at peace.

Do this for five to ten minutes.

Now imagine someone you know, love, and cherish. This may be your deceased loved one, or it may be someone else you feel close to. Try to choose someone who loves you or who has exhibited love toward you in the past.

As you think of this person, inhale and silently extend the following wish to this loving person:

May you be free from suffering.

As you exhale, silently extend the following wish to this person:

May you be at peace.

Do this for five to ten minutes.

Now imagine someone who has harmed you or your loved ones, someone whom you would consider an enemy. As you imagine this person, inhale and silently extend the following wish to this difficult person:

May you be free from suffering.

As you exhale, silently extend the following wish to this person:

May you be at peace.

Do this for five to ten minutes.

Now imagine your family. Extend your imagination to your community, your town, your state, and the country, extending it in every direction around you. Try to extend it further, imagining the entire planet, with all of its living beings. As you hold this visualization, inhale and silently extend the following wish to all beings:

May you all be free from suffering.

As you exhale, silently extend the following wish to all beings:

May you all be at peace.

Do this for five to ten minutes.

To finish the practice, open your eyes slowly. Take three more mindful breaths. Wiggle your fingers and toes, stretch out any limbs that may feel tight, and get up slowly.

✦ ✦ ✦

The Power of Loving-Kindness

I've been using this loving-kindness meditation to help people tap into their potential for compassion toward themselves and others for a long time. Several years ago, I was at a grief and bereavement conference and shared this exercise with participants. I didn't know exactly who all the attendees at my workshop were. I just knew that loving-kindness is a huge umbrella that everyone can fit under.

After my session was over, a fairly large group of attendees gathered around to introduce themselves. Many of them looked serene and at peace, which was quite different from how they came into the session. Many of them had tears in their eyes but were smiling. They introduced themselves as members of the Compassionate Friends, a network of bereaved parents who have lost children. It turned out that the attendees for my seminar were primarily people who had lost their children to homicide—someone had murdered their children. This is the most intense pain I can think of, and perhaps similar to the pain that's motivated you to read this book.

What these parents reported to me was that loving-kindness allowed them to feel closer to their children than they'd been able to for a long time. Sending loving-kindness to the murderer, something that completely defied logic, was actually liberating, allowing them to experience their memories of their children without the screen of hatred and anger at the murderer. Loving-kindness allowed them to feel a purer connection, one they didn't even know they had been missing.

This wasn't easy for them, and I doubt they would have attended the workshop had they known what we'd be doing. I probably wouldn't have thought loving-kindness was appropriate had I known who my audience was. This experience is a reminder that, in the situations where compassion is extremely difficult and least expected, it's often most powerful.

Although seemingly simple, loving-kindness meditation can have a transformative effect on your attitude. Loving-kindness can be one of the most powerful tools to help you through your grief—and any of life's challenges and surprises. Practice this technique as often as you can. I like to practice it at least once a week in addition to my daily mindfulness practice.

I find that loving-kindness has an extremely calming feel. I also find that it helps me think very differently about a lot of my relationships and interactions with people. It helps me not take my pain and frustrations too seriously, or at least not feel like I'm drowning in them by myself. It's amazing how focusing on sending other people good feelings can so easily help us feel soothed and less pain ourselves. I hope it has a similar healing effect for you as well.

Summary

One of the most challenging aspects of grief is losing a person who may have helped soothe you or who showed you the importance of closeness and togetherness. All too often, it's easy to become isolated by the pain of grief or the lack of good support. Loving-kindness practice can help you soothe yourself and reconnect with the healing power of relationships. It can also help you emotionally process any unfinished business with your loved one.

As you continue to develop your ability to soothe yourself with loving-kindness, reading the next chapter will help you discover other ways you can take control of your emotional well-being. The goal of using mindfulness with prolonged grief is to help you feel like you matter again and can take back your life from the depths of intense emotional pain. I believe that mindfulness and compassion are an ancient, tried-and-true foundation for human resilience. In the next chapter, we'll build on that foundation with some newer techniques from modern psychotherapy.

CHAPTER 9

✦ ✦ ✦

Creative Action

The mind craves permanence and predictability. It doesn't seem to particularly care about how you feel; it just wants to maintain the status quo, whether you're feeling happy, sad, angry, or well. When you suffer from grief or any other type of emotional pain for a lengthy period of time, it's all too easy to start feeling like you're stuck in a rut.

After a while, emotional pain becomes routine. This is a big part of what makes change so difficult. The pain has its own momentum, and the mind can easily get carried away down the road to persistent suffering. You begin to expect it, to assume that this is how you'll continue to feel because this is how you've been feeling. The pain doesn't seem like something that's happening to you anymore; it just feels like it's who you are. Grief and suffering can become your identity, rather than something you're enduring.

As a result, you're likely to act in ways that are consistent with how you feel and who you think you are. In this way, your pain can create deep-rooted assumptions that guide your behavior, and over time, how you feel can become who you are. As you know, time seems to go by more quickly the older you get. Before you know it, months, maybe even years, have gone by, and how you feel doesn't seem to have changed much. What has happened instead, unfortunately, is that this sense of the pain being who you are has solidified.

The Spiral Staircase of Grief

The spiral staircase is a metaphor I use to describe the natural ups and downs of grief that everyone experiences, hopefully with an upward momentum toward growth, integration, and expansion of identity. This is the natural course of grief, with the time frame varying widely from person to person.

The spiral staircase metaphor also captures the experience that grief can become much more intense around certain dates or times of the year. Typically, this occurs around holidays, birthdays, death dates, and the dates of other milestone events. I've found that, for many people, the anticipation of these milestones is harder than the actual date of the milestone event. This cyclical rhythm of grief during the calendar year is natural and normal when you understand it this way. The birth of a grandchild, a school graduation, or even the purchase of a new car—anything that can be considered a big deal or an important event—can inflame the suffering that grief can bring.

The pattern of prolonged grief is often quite different. Rather than being characterized by ups and downs, in prolonged grief your emotions may seem to hover around a very low emotional point, with more subdued ups and downs hovering around a lower emotional baseline. In essence, your grief remains at roughly the same level, spinning aimlessly rather than gradually rising and leading to growth. The result is a persistent, unrelenting blanket of emotional pain in the form of depression, anger, anxiety, or other unpleasant emotional states. This can have a huge influence on how you live your life, the decisions you make, and your expectations regarding your future.

Understanding the Links

Decades of research and clinical work in psychology have shown that behaviors are often guided by thoughts and feelings. How you think and feel will almost always directly influence how you behave and your choices about how to spend your time.

We also know that behaviors can, in turn, influence thoughts and feelings. So after painful emotions have persisted for a while, you can easily get stuck in a cycle in which negative thoughts generate negative feelings that guide behaviors that feed into more negative thoughts that lead to more negative feelings, and so on. Over time, these relationships between thoughts, feelings, and behaviors can become firmly entrenched. You may tell and retell yourself a narrative about who you are, how you're feeling, and how you're supposed to act to stay consistent with the script your mind is running nonstop. This is how thoughts, feelings, and behaviors can hover around a low emotional state for months or sometimes years on end if you don't make a deliberate and mindful effort to change them.

Challenging Assumptions

This relationship between thoughts, feelings, and behaviors is universal. It's not inherently either good or bad; it's just a pattern that we humans have. If you're prone to having underlying thoughts and assumptions that generate positive feelings, you're more likely to act in positive, compassionate ways. However, when you go through hard times in your life, such as the loss of a loved one, you may have underlying assumptions and thoughts that frequently generate distressing feelings and behaviors. Furthermore, the relationship between your thoughts, feelings, and behaviors may be preventing you from seeing alternative ways of being, even if you can't change what happened to you or other circumstances in your life.

I've seen this with patients hundreds of times. Solutions that might help them cope with difficult emotions and painful chapters in life can seem fairly obvious to outside observers but remain untried or perhaps even unimaginable to those distressed by grief. This isn't because the outside observers are smarter or because these patients are deficient in some way. We all tend to see things in a limited way that's consistent with our expectations of who we are, how we think the world operates, and what we expect from others.

These tendencies can cloud your judgment and impair your ability to transition from entrenched distress to well-being. We all tend to have certain expectations and assumptions about ourselves, the world, and others. These assumptions aren't always bad for us. Sometimes they help promote healthy behaviors and wholesome choices. Ultimately, assumptions exist because they're extremely efficient for the mind, just like that sense of control and permanence it craves.

It's only when these assumptions get in the way of living your life fully that they become problematic and promote suffering. Psychologist Jeffrey Young (Young and Klosko 1994) refers to assumptions that guide our behavior as schemas. They are like templates through which we see the world. Prolonged grief may trigger old, maladaptive schemas that feed off of other painful chapters in your life. For example, if you have an underlying schema that says you're unlovable, you may feel isolated and assume that it's useless to even try to be around other people, even people who might genuinely care for you or want to help you. If your schema is that no one can understand you, it's likely that you won't even bother to seek understanding or even companionship. Your mind may view behaviors that contradict schemas as a useless waste of time, thereby perpetuating your assumptions and further entrenching them.

The goal of working to develop greater clarity and insight into the relationship between your thoughts, feelings, and behaviors is to help you create a healthy schema that can become as firmly entrenched as the tendencies that are creating so much suffering for you. Mindfulness can help you become more aware of what your mind is chattering about and reveal your underlying assumptions so you can work through them. This clarity can empower you to choose active behaviors that allow you to take a more participatory role in your grief.

In the absence of this awareness, you may have a hard time engaging in behaviors that can change how you feel and perhaps help you feel better. Instead, underlying thoughts and feelings will continue to serve as barriers to taking action, whether that means deciding to declutter your home, telephoning a friend or family member who seems to care but stopped leaving messages when you didn't return calls, or going out to dinner with a new friend or acquaintance for the first time.

Cognitive Behavioral Therapy

The branch of psychology called cognitive behavioral therapy has pioneered in helping people with a variety of problems by working with the relationships between thoughts, feelings, and behaviors. I believe that mindfulness meditation and treatments based on mindfulness all qualify as types of cognitive behavioral therapy. Like cognitive behavioral therapy, mindfulness-based techniques rely on developing insight into how you think so you can break away from ways of thinking that don't serve you well or improve your life. Indeed, there is an ancient school of Buddhist psychology, called *abhidharma*, that explores the relationship between our underlying assumptions about reality and our behaviors.

At this point in working with this book, hopefully you have developed a somewhat regular mindfulness meditation practice and have been able to make some beneficial changes in your lifestyle, such as improving your sleep, diet, and level of activity. And ideally, in working with the previous chapter, you've developed a more compassionate attitude toward yourself and others. My goal in introducing mindfulness-based skills in this sequence is to help you become well acquainted with how mindfulness can transform major aspects of your life.

Most of the people I meet in my psychotherapy practice find it easier to gain deeper therapeutic insights once they've developed better ways of coping with their stress and pain. At this point in the book, you can now use the mindfulness skills you've learned and practiced to take a deeper look into how your mind works so you can generate more creative ways of living with prolonged grief.

✦ ✦ ✦ practice:
Tracking Assumptions and Generating Alternative Behaviors

One of the main tools I present in this chapter is a type of worksheet used by cognitive behavioral therapists to help clients develop better insight into their thoughts and feelings and how their behaviors can change once they've identified their underlying assumptions about life. The following chart is based on one that was devised by one of the founding fathers of cognitive behavioral therapy, Aaron Beck (Beck et al. 1979). I'd like to ask that you use this chart with your next five mindfulness sessions.

At the conclusion of these meditation sessions, think back to some of the thoughts and feelings you experienced during the session. Most people find it easier to identify a feeling and then trace the underlying thought, rather than trying to capture the thought first. So reflect on the feelings you experienced during the session, especially the unpleasant ones. Then use your mindful awareness to trace the thought that led to that feeling. (You may not have even realized you were having that thought.) Typically, these thoughts are associated with events that happened to you during the day or further back in the past. Record those events as well. Then identify what you normally do when you have these kinds of thoughts and feelings (behavior), and how you'd like to respond instead (alternative behavior).

As you'll see below, I also recommend using this approach with thoughts and feelings that come up in everyday life. A printable version of this chart is available for download at www .newharbinger.com; with it, you can track thoughts and feelings anywhere and anytime. Here's a sample to help you see how to fill out the chart.

Event	Feeling ("I was feeling…")	Underlying Thought ("I was thinking…")	Behavior ("I did…because of the way I was feeling.")	Alternative Behavior ("I would have felt healthier if I had done…instead.")
Grocery shopping	Anxious	I don't ever feel like I have enough time to do everything.	I rushed around and ended up forgetting to purchase some important things.	Try to do what I can as well as I can; next time, I'll bring a list.

Event	Feeling	Underlying Thought	Behavior	Alternative Behavior

Once you have some experience in tracking feelings and thoughts during your mindfulness practice, you can take the next step, which tends to be harder: tracking feelings in everyday life. For the next several weeks, use this chart to track some of the painful thoughts and feelings that arise, especially those that tend to arise frequently or that lead to behaviors that cause problems in your life.

Go ahead and start using the chart to track your feelings during different times of the day on different days. This type of tracking is at the heart of cognitive behavioral therapy. Much of what you've learned in this book has prepared you to engage in this tracking. As you've been reading and doing the practices, you've been developing nonjudgmental insight into your thoughts and feelings so that you can take more control over your behavior, hopefully helping you feel better in the process. Seeing your thought patterns on paper can give you a sense of what's driving your behavior and preventing you from engaging in preferable alternatives.

If you find using this chart beneficial, I recommend that you keep a copy at hand and complete it every night or at regular intervals. I find it extremely helpful whenever I'm at an emotional impasse and can't seem to move on. Many of my clients agree and use some form of this chart to help them sort out difficult feelings or identify what might be keeping them stuck in an unpleasant state.

After you've used the chart in daily life for a while, take a look at the "Alternative Behavior" column. Are the alternatives you come up with similar to those you identified when you were completing the chart during mindfulness sessions, or do they differ? Does doing the chart in either context encourage you more or help you feel healthier than using it in the other? Do your alternatives tend to feel more inspiring, empowering, or helpful in one context or the other?

Write the new behaviors in the "Alternative Behavior" column on a separate piece of paper or on index cards, and then post them somewhere you can see them regularly, like on your refrigerator door or bathroom mirror. Put them wherever they can provide inspiration and a gentle reminder that you do have choices in your behaviors. Remember, because of the interconnections between thoughts, feelings, and behaviors, heeding these reminders can help you break free of thought patterns that may be holding you back. You can use your alternatives like affirmations, to remind you that you can have some control over your behavior, and also over your thoughts and feelings.

✦ ✦ ✦

Creativity and Healing

When you develop the insight that comes from looking mindfully and clearly at the relationships between your thoughts, feelings, and behaviors, you open the door to making important changes in your life. In my view, a word that encapsulates meaningful, intentional change during suffering is "creativity." When you think of creativity, you may automatically think of painting, music, or sculpture. But you can bring creativity to just about any activity. Another way to think about creativity is that it's what happens whenever you think outside the box—outside of your usual automatic assumptions or habitual tendencies. In that light, whenever you express your feelings in a way other than how you typically do, you're being creative.

Intensely painful stories often lie behind works of art. Many of the finest paintings and most moving pieces of music have come from deeply painful events in artists' lives. If you analyze any of the top-forty popular music charts, you may be shocked at how many of the songs were composed around the time of a loved one's illness or death. You undoubtedly know how powerful music can be in bringing up memories. This may explain why musicians often use their craft to cope with their own pain and suffering.

That said, you don't have to be an accomplished singer, musician, or painter to benefit from creativity. I find that any chance people have to express their feelings in new ways can be extremely helpful. In the field of brain science, this helps foster what's called neuroplasticity, meaning the ability of the brain to form new connections between neurons. I believe that this is also intimately connected with healing. By making new connections between things that didn't seem connected before, all of life's experiences, including painful experiences, are integrated into a new coherent whole. This doesn't mean difficult experiences become pleasant or easy; they're just different and possibly a bit less painful or more manageable.

A lot of scientists think that behaviors that promote neuroplasticity might help slow down the aging of the brain, creating conditions similar to the time when we experience the most significant brain growth, as children (Esiri and Chance 2012). I don't believe it's a coincidence that early childhood is also the time when people tend to be most creative. Our society seems to grant permission to draw, use finger paint, make collages, or play with clay primarily to children. But we grown-ups can also benefit from creative expression. In fact, we may need it even more than kids do!

I believe that creativity and neuroplasticity also help facilitate resilience and recovery during some of the most difficult times in our lives. You can't be a kid again, but you can help wake up your brain's potential to be creative. I find that engaging in some extremely simple creative processes once in a while can be enough to help people feel rejuvenated, even if only temporarily, during the ups and downs and turmoil of prolonged grief. Think back to what you used to do as a child. Chances are, before the age of five, you spent a lot of time playing with clay or drawing; and, as you got older, you may have written short stories or poems, worked on jigsaw puzzles, or knitted. These activities helped your brain grow and adapt to your environment. There's nothing to say that you can't also use these creative modes of expression to help yourself now.

✦ ✦ ✦ practice:
Cultivating Creativity in Your Life

Creativity isn't just about finger painting, although it certainly can be! There are many different ways to keep the brain youthful, fresh, and resilient. In the list below, you'll find eighteen examples of ways to cultivate creativity. Any of them may help you see possibilities for being more creative in your journey with grief. As you read through these ideas, rank them in terms of how interesting or accessible they seem to you. For example, if attending a yoga class seems perfect, put a 1 next to that. If you find listening to different kinds of music to be the next most interesting thing, put a 2 next to that, and so on. Then, in the space next to each item, write about how you can practice that suggestion in your daily life. What kind of action plan do you need to put into place to make creativity happen?

Of course, you may not be able to do all of the items listed, but reviewing the list may give you a sense of the different approaches that can foster creativity in the healing process:

_____ Take a different route to frequent destinations. _____

_____

_____ Move the furniture around in one room of your house or apartment. _____

_____

_____ Learn a language. _____

_____

_____ Practice or learn to play a musical instrument. _____

_____

_____ Attend a yoga class. _____

_____

_____ Attend a dance class. _____

_____

_____ Attend an acting class. _____

_____

_____ Write poetry. _____

_____

_____ Begin an online blog. _____

_____

_____ Learn to draw or paint. _____

_____

_____ Make a drawing or painting. _____

_____

_____ Do sculpture or woodworking. _____

_____

_____ Plant flowers or plants or work in a garden. _____

_____

_____ Learn a new recipe. _____

_____

_____ Explore a local area you've never been to before. _____

_____

_____ Read about something you used to be interested in many years ago. _____

_____

_____ Listen to different kinds of music. _____

_____

_____ Spend time in nature. _____

_____

_____ Other: _____

_____

_____ Other: _____

_____

For many people, engaging in new, creative activities is facilitated by signing up for and attending an adult education class. These are usually held in local high schools, places of worship, and community colleges. Plus, in addition to helping you learn new skills, such as playing an instrument, ballroom dancing, or painting with watercolors, taking a class gives you an opportunity to meet new people.

If meeting new people sounds intimidating, just remember that you don't have to talk to anyone right away. However, when you do talk to classmates, you won't have to force the conversation—everyone is in the same class working on the same thing. And chances are, everyone is at a fairly similar skill level. You may also find that some of your classmates are also grieving, and that, like you, they are trying their best to be creative in the company of others.

If you prefer to do things on your own, creative activities—or simply applying creativity to the activities you already do—can give you a new way to spend your time. You may have spent so much time in the cocoon of your grief that your life feels stalled. Being more creative can give you the mental and emotional energy to process your grief a little differently and perhaps more directly. Personally, whenever I take out my colored pencils and drawing paper during a difficult time in my life, I feel as though I've made a new friend just because of the novelty of being creative.

✦ ✦ ✦

Summary

Sometimes grief comes from something so horrifying or traumatic that it seems impossible to meet it directly. In this situation, grief only very gradually becomes part of who you are. The pain can be so intense that it feels like it completely takes over your life and eclipses any meaningful growth that could come from your grief. Some of the insights that mindfulness can provide will help you generate alternatives to the path that your pain dictates. The practices in this chapter can help you develop more awareness of patterns of thoughts and feelings that may be serving as barriers to new behaviors, opening the door to finding alternative ways to manage your grief and other difficult emotions.

The next chapter, which is the last, will help you practice techniques that can help you target areas for growth in your journey with grief. This may sound strange. You may wonder how the intense pain of grief can possibly lead to anything like growth. Yet this is the challenge that confronts us all. The presence of intense emotional pain doesn't mean life pauses until you feel better; it certainly didn't ask for your permission before you experienced your loss. Therefore, you have to find ways to grow as you grieve, no matter how extensive or limited that growth may feel. Your life is still yours to live.

◆ ◆ ◆

CHAPTER 10

Mindful Resilience

G rief can be unpredictable. Like many distressing parts of life, grief can feel like it has a path of its own. You can feel lost, disempowered, and overwhelmed by normal daily tasks.

Hopefully this book has helped you find some tools to manage the stress of grief and take some healthy control of your life. You've been exposed to many ideas and techniques that can help you chart a holistic path toward better mental and physical health. You've learned and practiced mindfulness meditation and worked to improve your sleep, diet, and exercise. You've practiced skills to help you be more compassionate with yourself and others, and you've explored creative ways to approach your loss. You've also grown more intimate with how your mind works and how you can turn this insight into behavioral change.

All of the strategies and exercises in this book are intended to give you more of a voice in your grief, rather than being a victim of your loss. Bad things will happen in your life, and in everyone's life. That's a given. Nobody and no workbook can change that. But even though bad things have happened and may continue to happen, you can change your path in life. As you've learned in this book, some small but extremely significant steps can help you take control of parts of your life again.

Taking Charge

The mindful path through prolonged grief is about deliberately living as best as you can under profoundly painful circumstances. You may have found it impossible to "move on" or "get over it" as others may have suggested you should. With prolonged grief, that kind of advice is rarely helpful. A more realistic approach—and one that respects your individuality and the unique nature of your loss—is applying mindfulness to your experience and to taking charge of your life despite the lingering pain of grief. The mindful path through prolonged grief is about the process of living as fully as you can with the circumstances life has handed you. Your grief may not go away completely. But as it becomes part of who you are over time, you can make more decisions about who and how you want to be.

A New Perspective

Finding a new perspective is one of the biggest challenges in grief—and in any hardship you may suffer in life. We are conditioned to believe that bad things are all bad and good things are all good. It's difficult to comprehend that bad things can come from good, or that good things can come from bad. However, your pain and suffering have come from something good: loving someone. And from your pain, something meaningful and healing can emerge.

Even though you're suffering in your grief, you may grow from it. You can take charge of where and how you grow and what you need to do to make your journey one of growth.

Our minds usually prefer the simplicity of black-and-white thinking. You may idolize your deceased loved one because of this—something bad took your loved one away from you, and this injustice may amplify your sense of how undeserving your loved one was of what happened. It might seem as though your loved one was perfect, but unless people are very small children or babies when they die, it's usually possible to recall at least a couple of things that were unpleasant or annoying about them. This is how we all are and how all of our lives are. There are no simple answers; no one and nothing is all good or all bad.

Grief is no different. The emotions of grief can feel absolutely crushing and suffocating. You may have gotten used to your eyes being puffy first thing in the morning, your shoulders and jaw being tense and tight, your stomach feeling tied up in knots, or your joints being achy. These physical symptoms are all related to the stress of grief, and you can try to improve them. Grief may feel like a heaviness in your body and an altered state of consciousness in your mind, like a painful fog that just doesn't lift on some days. But something good can come out of that fog.

The Mindfulness Trajectory

Traditionally, one of the goals of mindfulness practice is to develop equanimity: an even-keeled disposition that can ride out the tumultuous waves of life's tough times. Mindfulness isn't a negation of life's ups and downs. It doesn't mean becoming numb, unfeeling, or boring. Rather, the hope is that mindfulness practitioners become more compassionate toward themselves and everyone around them and better able to embrace life's unpredictable ups and downs.

From its origins, mindfulness has been seen as the foundation stone for all spiritual growth and development. The Buddha, who was the first to openly teach mindfulness, said that our desires are constant and unceasing, and also that suffering is part of the natural order of our existence. You don't choose to be in pain; it finds you. But the Buddha also taught that practicing mindfulness can transform our experience of pain. In addition, it allows you to be present for any growth or meaningful changes that your pain and your grief may bring. Through the practice of mindfulness, something other than pain may emerge from your grief.

Working with Difficult Feelings

One of the most common yet most awkward emotions I've heard about from people who are grieving is feeling guilty for being relieved, sometimes even grateful, that their loved one is no longer suffering. Many people seem to feel that they should never feel good about something so bad. Yet this kind of relief is common, especially if a loved one experienced tremendous pain and suffering in the final weeks and months of life, or if the caregiving burden on the now-grieving loved one was exhausting and unsustainable.

Another feeling that can stand in the way of healing is the guilt you may feel about experiencing something fun, pleasant, or pleasurable after your loss, even months later, like a type of survivor guilt. Your mind may be telling you, *How dare you enjoy life when your loved one isn't here to share this with you!* Part of you might feel guilty because pleasant experiences seem to negate the memory of your loved one, contradicting the immensity of your loss.

Another common experience I've noted among people who have experienced trauma and intense loss is being ashamed about feeling abandoned by their spiritual beliefs and by God. If you feel this way, I encourage you to read about the experiences of others who have felt the same way. I always draw comfort from the writing of Viktor Frankl, who survived a World War II concentration camp and wrote a fantastic book called *Man's Search for Meaning* (1984). What's fascinating about Frankl's insights is that they are universally appreciated by clergy and atheists alike. He had a unique ability to speak to that gray area between faith and doubt, and his book may help you sort out some of your spiritual concerns without advocating one approach over another. What Frankl addresses is something even deeper than suffering: meaning.

Guidelines for Healing

Just as suffering is part of your life, so is healing. It seems that no one needs to make any effort to suffer. But healing takes deliberate effort, discipline, and practice. You aren't born knowing how to bounce back from tragedy and loss. You have to teach yourself. Part of how you can do so is by sitting with complicated feelings that feel contradictory, paradoxical, and unexpected. Some of these feelings, and some of the thoughts about these feelings, can get extremely complex. They often stand in the way of the growth that can happen after a loss.

However, just as your grief may serve as an emotional mausoleum, honoring your loved one, so can your healing. You don't need to hold yourself back from letting growth in a positive direction come from something so painful and distressing. Even though you're grieving, life keeps moving, and by now you may have some ideas of how you can deepen your awareness of what is happening to you and around you.

Loss is something that happens to you, but grief becomes something you do. You don't need to seek out this kind of suffering, but you do need to be an active participant in your grief. By practicing mindfulness as a way to navigate prolonged grief, hopefully you've learned that you can play an active role in your grief. The exercises in this book can continue to show you the steps you need to take to feel increasingly empowered in your grief and also help you see how far you've come. Grief often creates a filter of emotional pain that makes it hard, if not impossible, to see any sort of change or growth. Your emotions may have been so intense for so long that you don't have a sense of where you can take your grief or where your grief has taken you.

Again, the assumptions behind my approach are not to cross some imaginary finish line and be done with grief. Instead, I believe it is much more helpful and realistic to embrace the fact that the grief isn't going away on its own anytime soon; you have to find a way to live with it and even grow in it. This creates a context for figuring out what you can do about it.

I believe that setting goals for yourself during prolonged grief and other difficult times in life can help you get a sense of direction and also find meaning, in the way that Frankl found so helpful. It can help you determine where you're going and where you need to be. Like mountain climbers who set their sights on the peak they're hoping to climb, setting goals for your grief can create rallying points that will give you a sense of direction in life. All of the techniques in this book are meant to help you create goals for enhanced well-being and become more disciplined in acting in accordance with your goals.

In addition, mindfulness practices can help settle some of the painful rumination and other mental noise you're experiencing so you can devote more focus to the fullness and potential of each moment rather than being overwhelmed by pain. Mindfulness practices can also help alleviate some of the stress your body experiences due to grief.

✦ ✦ ✦ practice:
Assessing How Mindfulness Has Helped

In the following space, write about how your mindfulness practice and skills have helped you deal with your grief up to this point. Feel free to use a separate piece of paper if you need more space.

_____

_____

_____

_____

_____

_____

_____

_____

_____

_____

_____

_____

_____

Now write about how you'd like mindfulness to continue to help you. What more would you like your mindfulness practice to do for you? What goals do you feel mindfulness can realistically help you achieve in the coming year or so?

_____

_____

_____

_____

_____

_____

_____

_____

_____

_____

In chapter 9, I described how grief can feel like a spiral staircase. Although it feels like you're going in circles around certain dates on the calendar, when grief isn't prolonged, there's a general sense of upward growth, progress, or healing.

Prolonged grief can feel more like a maze, remaining much the same in its intensity as you travel paths that meander and go in different directions without much sense of progress or healing. The maze of prolonged grief can feel full of dead ends and false hopes. You may have a sense of stagnation in which grief has become an all-too-familiar and predictable part of your life. When you wake up in the morning during prolonged grief, you know exactly what you're going to be doing that day: grieving and suffering.

✦ ✦ ✦

Setting Goals in Grief

The techniques I'll present in this final chapter are designed to help give you a sense of progress, advancement, and healing, and, most importantly, a sense of direction. The pain of grief is universal, even though each person's experience of each loss is different. Every single one of us will grieve. You might as well use this pain to heal yourself and take control of your life again, step-by-step. For a lot of people, grief becomes a time of life when they build up a new identity and new sense of the world and their role in it. It can become—slowly, mindfully—a new beginning.

Psychologists call this *post-traumatic growth*. It is the ability to change or improve oneself in meaningful ways after horrible things happen. I love that phrase; it doesn't sugarcoat anything and is direct about what it's identifying. Post-traumatic growth is a counterbalance to post-traumatic stress. Both can exist in the same space; one doesn't necessarily negate the other. Unfortunately, few people in our society have a vocabulary for conveying this difficult concept: although you may still be suffering, that doesn't have to be all you're doing. I believe growth after loss is an essential part of the grief journey and within your reach.

Rebuilding Yourself

Our emotional states tend to become the stories we tell ourselves daily about who we are and who we're going to be. This mental chatter is constantly unfolding, and when you're practicing mindfulness, you develop an acute sense of how powerful it is and how much of your experience is created and perpetuated by this nonstop barrage of thoughts.

When you start to become mindful of how emotions make your body feel, you may be more likely to change the story you're telling yourself about yourself. This doesn't necessarily mean you can turn your grief off just by telling yourself a different story about yourself. Instead, as the mental chatter starts to change as a result of meditation and mindfully taking care of yourself, you may find yourself grieving less intensely from time to time.

One particularly powerful way to set empowering goals for change is to create a particular type of drawing called a *mandala*. In Asia, mandalas are drawings, usually circular, that depict a particular spiritual teaching or that symbolically map out the residence of a god or deity. In traditional Indian medicine, different parts of the body are depicted with different mandalas that express the particular properties of those parts of the body.

Mandalas convey a sense of wholeness and integration and can powerfully capture complex thoughts, emotions, or behaviors. Psychologist Carl Jung used mandalas extensively with his patients, and the following exercise is based on his work (1972).

✦ ✦ ✦ practice:
Drawing Mandalas

In this exercise, you'll draw images that come to your mind in response to various questions. Your drawings don't have to be complicated, and you don't have to be a great artist. Stick figures are fine. If you really can't draw, you can write down what you see instead. When filling in the blanks in the sentences below, you may wish to use a separate piece of paper so you'll have more room to write.

We've prepared blank sheets that you can use to complete this exercise; download them at www.newharbinger.com/27497. You'll also need a pen or pencil or, if you'd like to do this more elaborately, paint, colored pencils, or crayons.

Begin by placing the first sheet in front of you; then, practice mindfulness meditation for five minutes.

After meditating, fill in the blank in this sentence:

"I feel like my grief has been _____

_____."

Next, allow your mind to visualize an image that captures the phrase you wrote. Try to remember the first image that comes to mind.

Draw that first image inside the circle on the sheet of paper. Title this drawing "Past" in the space provided.

Next, practice mindfulness meditation for another five minutes.

After meditating, fill in the blank in this sentence:

"Today, I feel like my grief is _____

_____."

Next, allow your mind to visualize an image that captures the phrase you wrote. Try to remember the first image that comes to mind.

Draw that first image inside the circle on a second sheet of paper. Title this drawing "Present."

Next, practice mindfulness for another five minutes.

After meditating, fill in the blank in this sentence:

*"I would like my grief to change how I live my life by*_____

_____."

Next, allow your mind to visualize an image that captures the phrase you wrote. Try to remember the first image that comes to mind.

Draw that final image inside the circle on the third sheet of paper. Title this drawing "Future."

Take a look at all three mandalas. Is there a theme or underlying pattern that emerges in these drawings? Are your answers similar to your goals for your mindfulness practice? Do you see any progression, a direction of growth, or hope emerging from the journey through past, present, and future? If you find that the path isn't quite what you'd like it to be, try it again a little later on. You can do this exercise as many times as you like. You may wish to do it monthly or even weekly to help envision and record your goals for your journey with grief.

I recommend that you keep the mandala titled "Future" in a place where you'll see it regularly so it can serve as an affirmation and reminder of where you want to go. It can give you encouragement and hope in dark times. One day you may find that it speaks to you in a way you didn't anticipate.

This mandala depicting your future can remind you of your goals through your grieving process. Just as counting the breath in each mindfulness session helps focus the mind and track the practice, setting goals for your journey with grief can help you track your progress and growth. The circumstances of the loss you suffered may never be explainable, but your grief can be meaningful.

✦ ✦ ✦

Dedication of Merits

Traditionally, all Buddhist meditation practices and exercises were meant to be dedicated toward the welfare of all beings. This kind of compassion, called *dedication of merits*, has a wonderful effect on people who practice it in the midst of intense suffering. Practicing this can help you remember that you're connected to others, and that your suffering in grief is all too common and has been felt by billions of people over the course of human history.

Likewise, the potential for healing through grief has also been felt by just as many. In dedicating the merits of your mindfulness practice, you connect with the universal nature of suffering, but also the universal right to be healed from suffering.

For many meditators, setting compassionate goals seems like an obvious choice. After all, when you begin to practice nonjudgmental awareness of your own mind with a compassionate intent, it feels more natural to pass compassion on to others. In addition, compassion is good for you. In the midst of pain and suffering, thinking of the welfare of others can actually help you feel better by reducing your distress and boosting your immune system function (Pace et al. 2009).

✦ ✦ ✦ practice:
Finding Hidden Treasures

This practice will help you explore what you may have experienced in your grief aside from the obvious pain. The focus isn't on your pain and distress. Those are obvious, and as you know, you don't have to work at feeling the pain and suffering of grief. What generally does require some work is seeing the silver linings in grief, however small or faint they may be.

Let me be clear: This exercise is not about assuming good things have happened because of the loss you've suffered, or being glad you suffered in this way. This exercise is about finding out what you've learned about life and your abilities as a consequence of your grief.

This may be the first time you've done something like this, coaxing your mind to see something other than the pain and suffering you've experienced. This may be difficult for you to do. But without deliberate effort, it will be difficult to see anything but pain and suffering, even though there's usually more going on. This exercise can help you orient yourself and your mind toward post-traumatic growth.

I'll give you some examples of the silver linings people have shared with me in my clinical work. Perhaps some of them will sound familiar to you and help you get a sense of the silver linings you may have experienced as well. People have told me that they feel a deeper sense of how precious life, love, and relationships are. They've told me that they've received help and comfort from unexpected places, forging new friendships even as older ones disappoint and fade away. They've also said that they feel motivated to make sure that what they've experienced doesn't happen to others and therefore become advocates for social or legal changes or greater awareness of diseases or risk factors. Many people go on to form or lead support groups, reaching out to others who have suffered losses similar to their own.

You may feel grateful for new relationships. You might simply be grateful for some of the techniques you've learned in this book. You might feel grateful for being more present to fully experience the beauty of different aspects of nature, such as sunsets or the night sky. Perhaps you've found a new hobby, a new routine, or a new approach to life that feels soothing and helpful.

Even if none of these examples seems to match your experience, they can give you a sense of what post-traumatic growth looks like. This growth doesn't have to be the type that grabs headlines. Post-traumatic growth is often very private but powerfully transformative. Just as grief is unique and different for each of us, growth after loss is also unique. No two people will ever experience the exact same trajectory. The things you're grateful for will be unique to you and need not be dramatic or earthshaking to outside observers.

To help you get started with this way of thinking about life after loss, complete the following sentences. You may wish to use a separate piece of paper so you'll have more room to write.

My grief has taught me that life is about _____

_____.

The most helpful thing I've done in my grief is _____

_____.

The person most helpful to me in my grief has been _____

_____.

✦ ✦ ✦

✦ ✦ ✦ practice:
Setting Goals for the Coming Year

As you near the end of this book, I hope it has helped you, even if only just a bit. Take a moment to think back to how you were feeling when you started reading this book. How were things different?

Next, give some thought to what you're doing differently now. Then write down five things that you're glad you're doing differently. Perhaps some of these things stem from the practices you learned in this book or came about as a consequence of doing some of the exercises in the book. Perhaps some of them seem to be unrelated to the book. No matter how they seem to have originated, write these five things down in the following space:

1. _____

_____

2. _____

_____

3. _____

_____

4. _____

_____

5. _____

_____

Now write down five things you'd like to do differently in the coming year. Some or all of these may be the same as the items in the previous list. That's fine. Write them down anyway to help you remember and follow through on your insight:

1. _____

_____

2. _____

_____

3. _____

_____

4. _____

_____

5. _____

_____

This is what mindfulness in prolonged grief looks like: being aware of not just the pain of grief (that doesn't take any effort) but also of experiences other than pain. With mindfulness, you know that your grief is still there but that it can change, as all things do, and that you can change as well. Impermanence applies not just to death but to life, and also to the pain of grief. Mindfulness in prolonged grief is about being as connected to your life's potential as you are to life's pain and taking deliberate, mindful steps to manifest and experience that potential, even if only for a moment.

✦ ✦ ✦

✦ ✦ ✦ practice:
Charting Your Course

I've presented a lot of different practices in this book. Are there some that you've stuck with or found more rewarding than others? To help you remember everything you've learned, here's a list of all of the practices in the book:

- *Blue Sky Visualization*

- *Belly Breathing*

- *Using Cues for Belly Breathing*

- *Mindfulness Meditation*

- *Progressive Muscle Relaxation*

- *Passive Muscle Relaxation*

- *Variations of Body Scans*

- *Improving Sleep Hygiene*

- *Mindful Sleep Induction*

- *Lucid Dreaming*

- *Keeping a Dream Journal*

- *Moving Meditation*

- *Eating with Gratitude*

- *Eating Mindfully*

- *Preparing a Meal Mindfully*

- *Cleaning Up Mindfully*

- *Sweeping Mindfully*

- *Vacuuming and Decluttering Mindfully*

- *Exploring Your Relationship to Your Loved One's Belongings*

- *Exploring Whether Keeping Your Loved One's Things Is Problematic*

- *Mindfully Considering Your Loved One's Possessions*

- *Awakening Compassion*

- *Engaging in Random Acts of Kindness*

- *Metta, or Loving-Kindness, Meditation*

- *Tracking Assumptions and Generating Alternative Behaviors*

- *Cultivating Creativity in Your Life*

- *Assessing How Mindfulness Has Helped*

- *Drawing Mandalas*

- *Finding Hidden Treasures*

- *Setting Goals for the Coming Year*

In the space below, list the practices you've found most helpful, arranging them from most to least helpful:

_____

_____

_____

_____

_____

_____

Next, make a note of when you last did each of the most helpful practices:

_____

_____

_____

_____

_____

_____

In the following space, list which practices you'd like to do more often:

_____

_____

_____

_____

_____

_____

Devote some thought to how you can ensure that you do these practices more often, and then write your ideas in the following space:

_____

_____

_____

_____

_____

_____

_____

✦ ✦ ✦

The Way Forward

The mindful path through prolonged grief invites you to participate in your grief so you can build the best life you can, given what you've experienced. Grief has a purpose: it lets us know how powerful love is. When you lose a loved one, you are brought into sharp, merciless contact with how powerful relationships can be. What mindfulness teaches us is that awareness of each moment helps us understand our potential for living and loving despite this suffering.

The practices in this book are meant to help you become an active participant in your own life. Even though you've suffered, your life remains precious. Mindfulness can deepen your awareness of the precious potential each moment holds.

Treasure each moment.

Savor each sense.

Be present for each action, one moment at a time.

Dedicate your resilience to others.

References

American Psychiatric Association. 2000. *Diagnostic and Statistical Manual of Mental Disorders.* Washington, DC: American Psychiatric Association.

Beck, A., A. J. Rush, B. F. Shaw, and G. Emery. 1979. *Cognitive Therapy of Depression.* New York: Guilford Press.

Blumenthal, J. A., M. A. Babyak, P. M. Doraiswamy, L. Watkins, B. M. Hoffman, K. A. Barbour, et al. 2007. "Exercise and Pharmacotherapy in the Treatment of Major Depressive Disorder." *Psychosomatic Medicine* 69(7):587–596.

Blumenthal, J. A., M. A. Babyak, K. A. Moore, W. E. Craighead, S. Herman, P. Khatri, et al. 1999. "Effects of Exercise Training on Older Patients with Major Depression." *Archives of Internal Medicine* 159(19):2349–2356.

Bonanno, G., and K. Boerner. 2007. "The Stage Theory of Grief." *Journal of the American Medical Association* 297(24):2693.

Byock, I. 2004. *The Four Things That Matter Most: A Book About Living.* New York: Free Press.

Carlson, L. E., M. Speca, K. D. Patel, and P. Faris. 2007. "One Year Pre–Post Intervention Follow-Up of Psychological, Immune, Endocrine, and Blood Pressure Outcomes of Mindfulness-Based Stress Reduction (MBSR) in Breast and Prostate Cancer Outpatients." *Brain, Behavior, and Immunity* 21(8):1038–1049.

Chödrön, P. 1997. *When Things Fall Apart.* Boston, MA: Shambhala Publications.

Cuijpers, P., A. van Straten, L. Warmerdam, and G. Andersson. 2009. "Psychotherapy Versus the Combination of Psychotherapy and Pharmacotherapy in the Treatment of Depression: A Meta-Analysis." *Depression and Anxiety* 26(3):279–288.

Davison, K. M., and B. J. Kaplan. 2012. "Food Intake and Blood Cholesterol Levels of Community-Based Adults with Mood Disorders." *BMC Psychiatry* 12:10. doi: 10.1186/1471-244X-12-10.

Domhoff, G. W. 2003. *The Scientific Study of Dreams: Neural Networks, Cognitive Development, and Content Analysis.* Washington, DC: American Psychological Association.

Esiri, M. M., and S. A. Chance. 2012. "Cognitive Reserve, Cortical Plasticity, and Resistance to Alzheimer's Disease." *Alzheimer's Research and Therapy* 4(2):7.

Farb, N. A. S., Z. V. Segal, H. Mayberg, J. Bean, D. McKeon, Z. Fatima, and A. K. Anderson. 2007. "Attending to the Present: Mindfulness Meditation Reveals Distinct Neural Modes of Self-Reference." *Social Cognitive and Affective Neuroscience* 2(4):313–322.

Frankl, V. 1984. *Man's Search for Meaning.* New York: Washington Square Press.

Hoffman, S. G., A. T. Sawyer, A. A. Witt, and D. Oh. 2010. "The Effect of Mindfulness-Based Therapy on Anxiety and Depression: A Meta-Analytic Review." *Journal of Consulting and Clinical Psychology* 78(2):169–183.

Howell, A. J., N. L. Digdon, K. Buro, and A. R. Sheptycki. 2010. "Relations Among Mindfulness, Well-Being, and Sleep." *Personality and Individual Differences* 45(8):773–777.

Jacobson, E. 1938. *Progressive Relaxation.* Chicago: University of Chicago Press.

Jung, C. J. 1969. *Man and His Symbols.* New York: Doubleday.

Jung, C. J. 1972. *Mandala Symbolism.* Princeton, NJ: Princeton University Press.

Kabat-Zinn, J. 1990. *Full Catastrophe Living: Using the Wisdom of Your Body and Mind to Face Stress, Pain, and Illness.* New York: Bantam Dell.

Keys, A. 1995. "Mediterranean Diet and Public Health: Personal Reflections." *American Journal of Clinical Nutrition* 61(6):1321S–1323S.

Kearney, D. J., K. McDermott, C. Malte, M. Martinez, and T. L. Simpson. 2012. "Association of Participation in a Mindfulness Program with Measures of PTSD, Depression, and Quality of Life in a Veteran Sample." *Journal of Clinical Psychology* 68(1):101–116.

Kramer, A. F., S. J. Colcombe, E. McAuley, P. E. Scalf, and K. I. Ericson. 2005. "Fitness, Aging, and Neurocognitive Function." *Neurobiology of Aging* 26(suppl 1):124–127.

Kübler-Ross, E. 1969. *On Death and Dying.* New York: Simon and Schuster.

Kwan, B., S. Dimidjian, and S. L. Rizvi. 2010. "Treatment Preference, Engagement, and Clinical Improvement in Pharmacotherapy Versus Psychotherapy for Depression." *Behaviour Research and Therapy* 48(8):799–804.

LaBerge, S. 2009. *Lucid Dreaming: A Concise Guide to Awakening in Your Dreams and in Your Life.* Louisville, CO: Sounds True.

Maciejewski, P. K., B. Zhang, S. D. Block, and H. G. Prigerson. 2007. "An Empirical Examination of the Stage Theory of Grief." *Journal of the American Medical Association* 297(7):716–723.

Pace, W. W., L. T. Negi, D. D. Adame, S. P. Cole, T. I. Sivilli, T. D. Brown, M. J. Issa, and C. L. Raison. 2009. "Effect of Compassion Meditation on Neuroendocrine, Innate Immune, and Behavioral Responses to Psychological Stress." *Psychoneuroendocrinology* 34(1):87–98.

Pollan, M. 2009. *In Defense of Food: An Eater's Manifesto.* New York: Penguin Press.

Prigerson, H. G., M. J. Horowitz, S. C. Jacobs, C. M. Parkes, M. Aslan, K. Goodkin, et al. 2009. "Prolonged Grief Disorder: Psychometric Validation of Criteria Proposed for *DSM-V* and *ICD-11.*" *PLoS Medicine* 6(8):e1000121. doi:10.1371/journal.pmed.1000121.

Roemer, L., S. M. Orsillo, and A. Salters-Pedneault. 2008. "Efficacy of an Acceptance-Based Behavior Therapy for Generalized Anxiety Disorder: Evaluation in a Randomized Controlled Trial." *Journal of Consulting and Clinical Psychology* 76(6):1083–1089.

Shelton, R. C., and J. Fawcett. 2010. "Antidepressant Effects and Depression Severity." *Journal of the American Medical Association* 303(1):47–53.

Teasdale, J. D., Z. V. Segal, J. M. Williams, V. A. Ridgeway, J. M. Soulsby, and M. A. Lau. 2000. "Prevention of Relapse/Recurrence in Major Depression by Mindfulness-Based Cognitive Therapy." *Journal of Consulting and Clinical Psychology* 68(4):615–623.

Trungpa Rinpoche, C. 1993. *Training the Mind and Cultivating Loving-Kindness*. Boston: Shambhala Publications.

Young, J., and J. Klosko. 1994. *Reinventing Your Life: The Breakthrough Program to End Negative Behavior...and Feel Great Again*. New York: Plume Publishing.

Sameet M. Kumar, PhD, is a psychologist at the Memorial Healthcare System Cancer Institute in South Broward, FL, with over a decade of experience in working with end-of-life and bereavement. He is also the author of *Grieving Mindfully* and *The Mindful Path through Worry and Rumination*.

Foreword writer **Ronald D. Siegel, PsyD**, is assistant clinical professor of psychology at Harvard Medical School, coeditor of *Wisdom and Compassion in Psychotherapy*, and co-director of the annual Harvard Medical School Conference on Meditation and Psychotherapy.

FROM OUR PUBLISHER—

As the publisher at New Harbinger and a clinical psychologist since 1978, I know that emotional problems are best helped with evidence-based therapies. These are the treatments derived from scientific research (randomized controlled trials) that show what works. Whether these treatments are delivered by trained clinicians or found in a self-help book, they are designed to provide you with proven strategies to overcome your problem.

Therapies that aren't evidence-based—whether offered by clinicians or in books—are much less likely to help. In fact, therapies that aren't guided by science may not help you at all. That's why this New Harbinger book is based on scientific evidence that the treatment can relieve emotional pain.

This is important: if this book isn't enough, and you need the help of a skilled therapist, use the following resource to find a clinician trained in the evidence-based protocols appropriate for your problem.

Real help is available for the problems you have been struggling with. The skills you can learn from evidence-based therapies will change your life.

Matthew McKay, PhD
Publisher, New Harbinger Publications

new harbinger
CELEBRATING
40 YEARS

**If you need a therapist, the following organization
can help you find a therapist trained in cognitive behavioral therapy (CBT).**

The Association for Behavioral & Cognitive Therapies (ABCT) Find-a-Therapist service offers a list of therapists schooled in CBT techniques. Therapists listed are licensed professionals who have met the membership requirements of ABCT and who have chosen to appear in the directory.
Please visit www.abct.org and click on *Find a Therapist*.

Register your **new harbinger** titles for additional benefits!

When you register your **new harbinger** title—purchased in any format, from any source—you get access to benefits like the following:

- Downloadable accessories like printable worksheets and extra content

- Instructional videos and audio files

- Information about updates, corrections, and new editions

Not every title has accessories, but we're adding new material all the time.

Access free accessories in 3 easy steps:

1. Sign in at NewHarbinger.com (or **register** to create an account).

2. Click on **register a book**. Search for your title and click the **register** button when it appears.

3. Click on the **book cover or title** to go to its details page. Click on **accessories** to view and access files.

That's all there is to it!

If you need help, visit:

NewHarbinger.com/accessories

new harbinger
CELEBRATING
40 YEARS